ONE WEEK LOAN

Also available from Continuum

Teaching Happiness and Well-Being in Schools, Ian Morris

Future Directions, Diane Carrington and Helen Whitten

Meeting the Needs of Disaffected Students, Dave Vizard

Emotional Literacy, David Spendlove

7 Successful Strategies to Promote Emotional Intelligence in the Classroom,
  Marziyah Panju

Think Positively!

A course for developing coping skills in adolescents

Erica Frydenberg

Resources to accompany this book are available online at: http://education.frydenberg.continuumbooks.com

Please visit the link and register with us to receive your password and to access these downloadable resources.

If you experience any problems accessing the resources, please contact Continuum at: info@continuumbooks.com

continuum

Continuum International Publishing Group

The Tower Building   80 Maiden Lane, Suite 704
11 York Road   New York
London   SE1 7NX   NY 10038

www.continuumbooks.com
http://education.frydenberg.continuumbooks.com

British Library Cataloguing-in-Publication Data
A catalogue record for this book is available from the British Library.

ISBN: 978-1-4411-2481-4 (paperback)

Library of Congress Cataloging-in-Publication Data
A catalog record for this book is available from the Library of Congress.

Typeset by Ben Cracknell Studios
Printed and bound in Great Britain by Ashford Colour Press Ltd, Gosport, Hampshire

Contents

Foreword
by Tom Oakland

I was excited to receive and read *Think Positively!* Dr Erica Frydenberg and I live about 10,000 miles apart, so I see her only occasionally at international conferences. Nevertheless, I have developed a deep appreciation for her scholarly and personal qualities. I knew the book would reflect these qualities and my excitement was rewarded in reading her book.

Human behaviour displays that wonderful quality of associating new learning with what we already know and believe. For example, we all have read passages in books that introduced some new ways of thinking, leading us to wonder whether these related thoughts will be reinforced through later passages. If they aren't reinforced, we tend to be disappointed and will often put the book to one side. If we find our related thoughts reinforced through subsequent passages, we feel we are walking hand and hand with the author. I had this experience in reading *Think Positively!*

I wrote marginal notes as I read the Introduction. The book's contents brought ideas of the impact of emotional intelligence on our social and emotional behaviours –including our happiness, the mind–body connections characterized in executive control, the beneficial effects of cognitive behaviour therapy – one of the most scientifically supported treatments in psychology, Seligman's captivating notions of positive psychology and the weaving of science and practice. When I finished the Introduction and began reading other chapters I found these, and other initial ideas, reinforced and I really felt I was walking hand and hand with the author as she guided me in new and helpful directions.

For years I avoided the topic of coping, as I believed that coping was doing the best with the hand we are dealt – a belief often shrouded by dark clouds. Dr Frydenberg's earlier scholarship on this subject helped me see coping in a new light, one that moved from being a victim of one's circumstances to having considerable control over one's self and environment.

I grew up with the belief that our success or failure is governed strongly by our expectations and hard work. Psychological science confirms that our chances of success improve significantly when we anticipate success and work toward it.

As a psychologist I have come to appreciate the impact of three qualities on human behaviour: our biological basis, our environments and our personal choices. Children and teenagers have little control over the first, some control over the second and considerable control over the third. *Think Positively!* emphasizes the importance of making good personal choices and provides concrete strategies to acquire and sustain them.

Dr Frydenberg's work has removed coping from the shadows by casting it in new and engaging ways, ones that resonate with the belief that we need to establish a healthy and positive vision for ourselves, a plan to achieve it and expectations our vision will be achieved through persistent personal effort and work.

Another of the strengths of *Think Positively!* is that it is embedded in psychological sciences, thus dispelling the idea that the book's message belongs in the feel-good, self-help section of a book store. Dr Frydenberg nicely weaves some of the latest scholarship from cognitive, neurocognitive, social, developmental, educational and related psychological science to form a basis for her theory – and, importantly, her proposed intervention methods.

Her work is intended to have multiple outcomes for a wide age range. These include understanding the importance of coping methods to deal with stress, current scholarship on positive methods to deal with stress and the importance of proactively establishing personal goals and working hard to achieve them. So the implications of her message are important for everyone and this book has universal appeal.

It may be more important for her main audience: teenagers. Their brains are becoming rewired to assist them in thinking like adults, rather than children. Their social and emotional qualities need to move from upheaval to stability. The teenage years tend to be the most turbulent and to present more new life challenges than at any other time, so the emphasis of *Think Positively!*, to provide a curriculum that helps teenagers to acquire healthy coping strategies and so to move successfully from childhood to adulthood, is commendable.

Its 12 modules address steps needed to acquire and retain beneficial coping skills. Examples include acquiring needed language, thinking positively, getting along with others, solving problems, making decisions, setting and attaining goals and managing time. I am particularly grateful for guidance on ways to develop coping styles with children who experience divorce, depression, learning problems and chronic illness and those diagnosed with Asperger's.

Dr Frydenberg has developed an international reputation for her important scholarship on coping and this is reflected in this book. Her strong convictions about the importance of coping are seen in her personal qualities, ones characterized by intimacy, building capacity, happiness, health, hope, life success, originality, positive approaches, resilience, self-efficacy, spirituality and wellbeing. The flow of one's pen, when discussing these qualities, is made easier when one personally embraces them.

Thomas Oakland
Professor, University of Florida
President, International Foundation for Children's Education

Acknowledgements

This book is dedicated to the many educational psychology students who have graduated from the Educational Psychology Unit at University of Melbourne since the early 1990s. They have contributed to the field of coping in numerous ways through their research and practice. They have advanced our understandings of young people's coping and have enriched my life in so many ways. I have enjoyed working with them and have drawn great satisfaction from their accomplishments.

There are some who warrant particular mention. Kelly O'Brien, whose enthusiasm and practitioner insights have made it a joy to work with her in developing some of the coping skills modules, and whose excellent clinical work with a depressed adolescent has contributed insights on how the concepts may be adapted in a one-on-one setting. Chelsea Eacott, has researched and practised in the field of coping whilst at the University of Melbourne and was able to assist with the text. Nola Firth whose important research and contribution relating to coping skills development of learning disabled young people is appreciated. The excellent and innovative contribution of Cecilia Wing Chi Lam, who has developed and evaluated coping skills to assist young people to deal with the cyber world in Module 10, is acknowledged. Clare Ivens has also researched the field of coping, particularly in relationship to children of divorce, a topic to which she has contributed in Section 3. Her contribution to Module 6, dealing with anger, is also acknowledged. Helen Evert has drawn on her experience of working with young people who have Asperger's and her contribution to that topic in Section 3 is appreciated. Finally, the contributions of Catherine Brandon, who worked extensively on *The Best of Coping* almost a decade ago, and my colleague Professor Ramon Lewis, who has been a collaborator on the development of the coping constructs and the theoretical insights into the coping process, are acknowledged. It is those insights that have informed what underscores this volume.

Kathryn Kallady's editorial assistance during the final stages of the manuscript preparation is appreciated.

My family, Harry, Joshua, Lexi, Adam, Oscar and Claudia provide the joy that propels me to continue my endeavours in the field of coping, with adults, adolescents, children and more recently with children in the pre-school years. I am truly appreciative.

Introduction

Staying on top

Today there is flurry of interest in health, wellbeing, happiness and developing resilience to cope with whatever life dishes out. There is no evidence to say that we were happier 20 or 50 years ago but there is also no evidence to the contrary, that is, that we are less happy. However, there have been increases in the reported rates of self-harm, depression, suicide and substance abuse. To turn these around we will need to tip the balance from despair and poor wellbeing to more positive ways of valuing and enjoying our time on the planet.

Ed Diener, University of Illinois' father of the study of wellbeing, points out that while there is no single factor that makes everyone happy, there is a range of strategies that are supported by research that can contribute to achieving happiness. They are both cognitive and action based. These include the capacity to relate to others, to make others happy, to achieve intrinsic enjoyment from one's pursuits and the ability to become optimistic. All these capabilities can be learnt. Thus we have the capacity to 'tip' the current thinking and focus on depression to one of capacity building in all areas that relate to human resilience and wellbeing.

Health, happiness and success in life are related to the development of psychosocial competence, one aspect of which is coping. In contrast to books that have made their starting point the identification of illness or psychosocial problems this book focuses on the development of health and competence. It is in line with current developments in psychology that are focused on a positive approach, health, wellbeing, optimism and self-efficacy, that is, the belief in one's capacity to cope. There will be an emphasis on providing skills for the individual learner as well as for the instructor.

This book is underpinned by cognitive behavioural principles that are in turn underscored by research evidence and these principles have been utilized to develop the instructional modules and worksheets.

The book has three sections. Section 1 describes the contemporary influences of positive psychology, coping theory and measurement that provide the tools and language for the development of instruction in coping skills. Section 2 details the 12 modules of the programme that have been developed for universal applications, that is, in settings such as regular classrooms. Section 3 describes the diverse applications in the classroom and in clinical settings as well as providing examples of adaptations which have been implemented and which may provide the stimulus for further adaptations to meet the needs of a particular population or setting.

The positive psychology movement has generated great interest that has resulted in a rapid growth around the world, and is arguably the most exciting developments in psychological theory and practice in the last decade.

From depression to empowerment

Depression is being experienced in 'epidemic' proportions in many Western communities and, in particular amongst young people. The search for effective ways to reverse this trend has resulted in a significant shift in psychological approach from a focus on helplessness and pathology to a more positive orientation that emphasizes health and wellbeing. This shift is evident in the literature. Much has been written about optimism and empowerment and how these contribute to an understanding of how we confront the challenges of life, develop goals and visions and attain success.

There are many challenges to be faced in contemporary society, including the stresses of everyday living in the technological age and changes in patterns of employment and family life. How we respond to these challenges to achieve a successful outcome from the perspective of the individual is of major interest. The fostering of personal agency is an important component in 'inoculating' both adults and young people against depression.

The field of positive psychology aims to promote positive emotions, positive character traits and positive institutions. Its emphasis on the enhancement of positive phenomena represents a significant break from mainstream psychology, which generally aims to eliminate negative phenomena such as mental disorder and prejudice. Its reliance on scientific research methods and its rigorous evidence base also sets it apart from 'popular' and humanistic psychologies. At the level of subjective experience, positive psychology focuses on wellbeing, contentment, life satisfaction, happiness, flow and hope. At the level of personality traits, it aims to cultivate strengths and virtues such as love, courage, aesthetic sensibility, perseverance, forgiveness, originality, spirituality and wisdom. At the societal level it aims to advance civic virtues and the institutions that move individuals toward better citizenship: responsibility, nurturance, altruism, civility, moderation, tolerance and work ethic.

Some of the outcomes of positive psychology in an education setting include allowing individuals to:

❀ Enhance resilience, positive emotions, stress management and wellbeing
❀ Identify and develop character strengths

❀ Build engagement in the classroom and beyond
❀ Increase optimism and gratitude
❀ Promote positive communication and positive relationships
❀ Improve performance and productivity

All these are goals of the coping skills programme.

Since the mid 1960s and particularly in the last decade there has been a concerted effort to determine how individuals deal with stress, that is, coping. In order to foster healthy social and emotional development we need to change the language of despair to a language of optimism and ability. Talking about coping is a step in the right direction. How people think to a large extent determines how they feel. A greater capacity to reflect on one's situation and assess or develop the appropriate responses to a particular circumstance is most important. The development of coping language along with coping skills holds promise for the future.

Assessment of coping through the use of psychometric tools has led to the development of a growing number of instruments for use with adolescents. The Coping Scale for Adults (CSA) (Frydenberg & Lewis, 1997) and the Adolescent Coping Scale (ACS) (Frydenberg & Lewis, 1993a) developed in the Australian context and used by thousands of people, both in Australia and in many communities outside Australia, provide a way of assessing how an individual copes and provide a language of coping. It allows young people to develop their coping profile on a valid and reliable instrument and to reflect on their coping. Through completing a questionnaire, adolescents are introduced to the language of coping and the many different ways of coping. They are then open to reflection, teaching and personal change. While these instruments and the inherent constructs provide a backdrop for the coping skills programmes and are available for professionals with a psychometric background, this volume provides a simplified, user-friendly format to introduce users to the language and concepts inherent in the programme. While a psychometrically validated instrument may be used, particularly as a before and after measure, it is not essential. It is the conceptual areas that are detailed in Module 1 (see page 26) that are the important underpinnings of coping skills instruction. These conceptual areas with their exemplars can be listed and the usage rated against a 1–10 scale to indicate which strategy is used a lot and which is used a little. These sorts of ratings can in turn be used as a pre- and post-measure of the coping programme.

The principle that underscores the coping skills programme is that we can all do what we do better. If we do not like how we cope in certain contexts we can learn new strategies. It is possible to enhance and develop one's coping if we have a framework within which to do that. Thus the programme is a universal one and instructors will bring their own experience and adaptations to the modules.

The modules

Section 2 details the 12 modules and has been designed to help adolescents identify, reflect upon and develop their current coping style. The main purpose of the programme is to facilitate the learning of positive thinking skills and the development of productive coping strategies to adolescents. The programme encourages students to understand that there are different ways of coping and that some coping strategies may be more useful than others.

The programme includes topics that relate to 'the language of coping', 'productive and non-productive coping', 'relationship building', ' dealing with conflict', 'goal setting', 'goal getting', 'problem-solving', 'asking for help', 'time management', and 'assertiveness training'. The programme should be delivered in a fun and creative way. The many activities, some for classroom groups and others that can be followed as homework activities, have clear instructions.

Thus the generic programme aims to build resilience in young people by allowing them to explore how they deal with different situations, problems and worries that come up in their own lives. The programme does this by allowing students to identify their own coping strategies, evaluate these strategies in terms of whether they are productive or non-productive, as well as identify alternative strategies for different situations so that individuals are better able to cope with the demands placed on them. In addition the programme also allows students to build their skills in the following areas: communication, problem-solving, decision-making, goal setting, and who to go to for help.

The programme is comprehensive but sufficiently flexible to enable it to be used in various settings with young people who have different needs. Generally modules 1, 2, 3 and 4 should be offered sequentially and as foundation modules for the subsequent parts of the programme. Module 1 provides an introduction to the theoretical framework and language of coping which are utilized in many of the subsequent modules. Module 2 helps young people become aware of the ways in which they can change the way they think and subsequently how they appraise events (positively or negatively), and how they cope. Module 3 has an emphasis on what not to do. The evidence is emerging very clearly that when it comes to coping it is important to teach young people what not to do as much as what to do. It is the use of the 'non-productive' coping strategies such as 'worry', 'self-blame' and 'tension reduction' that are most readily associated with depression. Module 4 emphasizes communication skills which play an important part in effective interactions. Asking for help depends on the capacity to communicate effectively and forms the basis of Module 5.

The subsequent seven modules – Coping with conflict, Problem-solving, Social problem- solving, Decision-making, Coping in cyberworld, Goal setting and goal setting, and Time management – provide an essential set of skills, but in a particular setting some may be more relevant than others. However, it is suggested that Module 12 (Time management) be dealt with after Module 11 (Goal setting and goal getting) as it becomes more relevant when students are able to draw upon experiences considered in the earlier module.

Each of the modules targets the development of coping skills for adolescents and provides information on a particular aspect, and includes self-reflection activities and a quiz.

Section 3 details what we have learned through various applications of coping skills training. Additionally it addresses some adaptations that have been made to date or are being made so that the reader will benefit from the numerous ideas and possibilities that have been tried when teaching coping skills within the framework presented in the 12 modules. These include learning disabled, those who have experienced loss, divorce or depression, young people with diabetes and young people with Asperger's Syndrome. These adaptations are by no means comprehensive but are presented as exemplars of applications and as a stimulus for instructors to consider when requiring an application for a particular group.

How the modules are to be used

The modules been designed for a universal population of 12–18 year olds. However, much of the content has been found to be suitable for 'gifted' or highly able groups of young people who are several years younger. Similarly, the content can be simplified for a less able population of older adolescents. While the programme is quite fully scripted, it is possible to deviate from the script and bring on board examples that apply to a particular population. While the universality of the concepts should make it readily applicable to different contexts and cultures represented by different populations of young people, it is always important to use examples that are relevant to a particular population.

The programme can be offered in small or large groups, depending on the need and the confidence of the instructor. In a large group, a teacher's assistant is highly desirable. There are group activities and students can complete some tasks in a designated workbook which can be created for personal use. Additionally there are individual activities that can also be completed in the school setting or as homework activities. While sharing of ideas is to be encouraged, students need to feel safe in the environment and to disclose only what they feel comfortable doing. Nevertheless there should be an understanding in each group that what is discussed in the group stays within the group rather than becoming public information.

The modules have been designed for a 40–50 minute classroom period but with some groups it may take longer to learn and reinforce the concepts. Weekly modules enable the programme to be covered in a school term and the staggering of the modules is recommended to enable maximum rehearsal and reinforcement to occur. However, it is possible to administer the programme during an intensive period such as a school camp or summer programme. If this is the preferred format then it is recommended that booster activities be provided to remind students of the concepts. This can be done in the form of revision and revisiting of modules or through the use of a CD-ROM such as *Coping for Success*, available through the Australian Council for Educational Research. Regardless of whether it is the staggered or intensive programme format that is used, it has been found to be highly desirable to revisit the instruction three, six or 12 months later.

SECTION 1

Positive psychology, cognitive behavioural theory and the field of coping: what we know

Psychology has had a long history, from the nineteenth to the twentieth and now to the twenty-first century. We continue to learn from the past and add new insights and perspective in the present. Where we stand in the twenty-first century is a progression from the unconscious processes that dominated psychology in the late nineteenth and early twentieth centuries –Sigmund Freud (1894) and the unconscious, James (1892), understanding of the self, and Galton (1883), introspection – through to behaviourism (Skinner, 1953; Wolpe, 1958) and the cognitive revolution (Beck, 1993; Ellis & Harper, 1975; Meichenbaum, 1994, 1977), and the appreciation of the power of the mind and the way that cognitions or our thinking can change the way we feel and act.

The early years of the twenty-first century have also given rise to the positive psychology movement, primarily led by Martin Seligman (1992), whose own work has moved from a learned helplessness model to one of capacity, hope and optimism. We are now encouraged to see the world in terms of our capacities rather than our inadequacies. Another encouraging development that has fuelled optimism is the knowledge that has been provided by neuroscience through the growing evidence that the brain continues to develop through adolescence and beyond, and is able to change itself to compensate for loss or deficits (Doidge, 2007).

Cognitive behaviour therapy

The behaviourist schools, along with the cognitive revolution, have led to a range of therapeutic approaches gaining prominence. They can be grouped under the term Cognitive Behaviour Therapy (CBT), an approach that focuses on changing the way we think about events and how that thinking impacts our behaviour. Additional terms have been introduced, such as Rational Emotive Therapy (REBT), introduced by Albert Ellis who emphasized challenging and correcting maladaptive thinking. What CBT and REBT have in common is that they deal with the 'here and now' rather than the past, the conscious rather than the unconscious, and there is evidence for tangible beneficial outcomes following the therapeutic intervention.

While not everyone needs individualized or group therapy, therapeutic techniques in themselves can be used for universal instruction as they draw heavily on the principles of behaviourism and cognitive psychology, which are all part of good education and learning. An additional, strong feature of CBT, as with any instructional activity, is the capacity to establish that learning has occurred. That is, the approach can be considered to be grounded in evidence both in practice and outcomes.

Thus this conceptualization and subsequent clinical treatments have found widespread acceptance as evidence-based interventions for numerous disorders, particularly those relating to anxiety and depression. Furthermore, since one in five young people in Western communities such as the UK, USA and Australia is expected to experience at least one significant stress in their lifetime (WHO, 2007), it is important to equip young people to deal with the stresses that they may encounter.

The positive psychological movement has provided the impetus for extending the application of these principles towards achieving psychosocial health and wellbeing, along with benefits that accrue for the achievement of success. It is the principle that we *can* change the way we *think* and subsequently the way we *feel* and *act* that underscores *Think Positively!* While the theoretical framework of the volume is cognitive behavioural, the programme is also underpinned by coping theory. Coping theory addresses the skills that are required to deal with the demands of everyday life and with major stresses when they arise. Additionally, coping skills go beyond adaptation to assist the individual to do more than survive, that is, to thrive.

The adolescent brain

The long-held view that adolescents are different from adults in a number of respects is readily accepted. Adolescents can perform in remarkable ways in terms of cognition and learning as well as being enthusiastic, energetic, caring and concerned about a range of socially important issues. At the same time they are often limited in their capacity to control impulses and are not likely to plan their decision-making. More recently, it has been recognized that some of these limitations are due to the adolescent brain being a 'work in progress'. The wiring becomes 'richer, more complex and more efficient' (Weinberger, Elvevag & Giedd, 2005). The prefrontal cortex, often referred to as the 'CEO' or executive of the brain because it is responsible for higher order skills, is in a state of development with both pruning and growth occurring.

Technology such as Magnetic Resonance Imaging (MRI) allows close observation and mapping of the brain during emotional responses to a particular situation, or when part of the brain has been damaged. Despite a great deal of neuro-scientific knowledge being grounded in research, the relative contribution of genetic and environmental factors is not known. What is known is that there is growth and development which provides an opportunity for teaching and intervention (see Weinberger, Elvevag, & Giedd, 2005). Since we know that the adolescent brain is undergoing change and development, this provides us with major opportunities to impact cognitive growth and learning. It is an optimum time to utilize the educational setting to facilitate social and emotional growth.

Social and emotional learning

Social and emotional competence includes key qualities which, when put into practice, produce socially and emotionally healthy and productive individuals, as well as safe and responsive communities. Qualities include reflection and empathy, flexible and creative problem-solving and decision-making, control of impulses, clear and direct communication and self-motivation. There is a vital role for education in enabling positive social and emotional development of young people and the adults around them. There is a significant body of research demonstrating a strong link between social and emotional wellbeing, educational outcomes and the critical role of social and emotional wellbeing across the lifespan.

❀ There is evidence that these skills can be taught from preschool to Year 12
❀ Students participating in effective social and emotional education programmes characteristically engage in less self-destructive and disruptive behaviour and in more positive social behaviour
❀ Furthermore, they often show improvements in their academic performances (Weissberg, 2007)

The challenge

The challenge is how to skill young people to meet the unprecedented stresses and strains in their lives. Some of the factors which contribute to the stresses and strains experienced by young people include:

❀ The breakdown of the traditional family structure
❀ The impact of globalization, with more families moving around the country and abroad in search of work opportunities
❀ Longer working hours for those in employment
❀ Higher unemployment rates, particularly in rural areas
❀ Various pressures on the family unit, affecting the emotional and financial security of family members
❀ The advent of new technologies which has taken away a lot of the manual labour from our work places, thereby reducing vocational opportunities for those with lesser qualifications
❀ Pressures on young people to succeed and the need for them to meet higher qualification requirements in order to get jobs
❀ The projection of violence into our lives, particularly through the media
❀ A growth in obesity in young people which, when coupled with the greater emphasis on image and beauty, increases the stress on our youth to be 'accepted'
❀ The decline of religious institutions as a source of moral and communal support
❀ The ebbing away in some areas of professional resources, caused by rationalization of services in the public and private sectors

Each of the stresses and strains described above, either alone or in combination, contributes to the challenges facing schools and put demands on them to play a more active role in nurturing the social emotional development of young people. Increasingly, schools are dealing with these problems, either because they see a young person in need, because the community has turned to them for help or because there is an expectation that schools should meet these adaptational needs of young people in preparation for their future lives.

There is a high cost to the community of a failure to meet the ever-growing demand for support. The estimates indicate that up to 20 per cent of young people will experience mental health-related difficulties during their school years (WHO, 2009). The costs in student distress, educational under-achievement and the utilization of interventions that require medication is known to be high. Common forms of intervention include a range of medical and psychological interventions. However, the most ideal option is prevention, as it is a healthy, resilient population that we are endeavouring to develop.

Some programmes are generic in that they attempt to build resilience in a general sense. *Thinking Positively!* is preventative in nature as well as dealing with those who are presently not coping and are in need of rehabilitation. In essence, it is designed to help the young people of today to take responsibility for themselves – to notice their problems and deal with them before they become too severe. Self-help is ultimately the best coping strategy.

Schools provide an opportunity for systematic training in social emotional competence during the 12–13 years that they are educating young people and linking that to educational outcomes. Social and emotional competence provides a firm foundation for human endeavour, achievement and a healthy community. Coping skills are an important index of such competence. Finding the best ways to promote productive coping and reduce the reliance on non-productive coping strategies by young people is a fundamental social challenge for schools and policy makers.

There is substantial research currently taking place in the field of coping. In particular, there are some exciting developments, in that we are getting to understand what to teach and what not to teach, what the common features of effective programmes are and what elements of school structures support prevention activities. We know a great deal about the best way to promote social and emotional programmes, such as coping, in schools. First, bringing on board teachers and instructors who are enthusiastic and willing to teach such a programme; secondly, training teachers and instructors prior to programme implementation; thirdly, providing support for teachers from professionals such as school psychologists while they implement the programme; and, fourthly, introducing the programme to a whole class, so that all students benefit and those needing these skills most are not grouped together or singled out. Regardless, those most in need are likely to benefit the most.

From stress to coping

The first date, sitting an exam or a visit to the doctor, being away from home. It is clear that the same event is not experienced in the same way for each individual. For some, there is joy and anticipation while, for others, there is anxiety and fear of the encounter. What is stressful for one person is not stressful for another. It is the perception or appraisal of the event that impacts on both the experience and the response.

There are readily recognized symptoms of stress such as reluctance to go to school, headaches, stomach aches and eczema and more masked expressions of stress, such as bullying, disruption in the classroom and sleeping disorders (see Youngs, 1985; Compas, 1987). While the manifestations of stress may be familiar, the causes, extent and severity are not always clear.

The term 'stress' has its origins in physics rather than in psychology and physiology. Essentially, it was a term used in engineering to describe the effect of a mechanical force that placed strain or pressure on an object. The physiological theories of stress focus on the arousal that occurs when an organism is under stress or threat and there is a response to that stress which may be adaptive, in that there is an attempt to 'fight' or 'flee' the stress. When the stress persists there is likely to be a harmful outcome for the organism (Cannon, 1932). More recently there has been a challenge to this traditional view of stress as research has shown that a more typical female response to stress has been labelled 'tend-and-befriend' (Taylor, Kline, Lewis, Gruenwald, Gurung & Updegraff, 2000). Under stress the female response is directed at maximizing the survival of the self and the offspring through nurturing, protecting the offspring from harm and affiliating with others to reduce risk.

Illness is often a result of the exertion or demand that is made on a particular physiological system. Biological or genetic predisposition may play an important part in illness. Selye (1976) described stress as developing from 'the non-specific response of the body to any demands' (page 472). Selye makes the distinction between stress which mobilizes the individual to effective performance – 'eustress' – such as when there is heightened performance in an exam and stress which is more negative and has been labelled 'distress'. Lazarus (1974) describes stress as the mismatch between the perceived demands of a situation and the individual's assessment of his or her resources to deal with these demands. Stresses can be physical, such as those pertaining to the environment, like extreme heat or cold, or psychosocial, such as relationships that are not working and daily hassles, such as having a quarrel with one's friend.

Since the mid 1960s, and particularly in the last decade, there has been a concerted effort to determine how individuals deal with stress, that is, coping. The adult research and theorizing has generated models of theory and practice that have been readily adapted for use with children and adolescents.

Theories of stress and coping in adolescents have evolved from an adult-centric orientation and the assumption has been that they apply in much the same way in childhood and adolescence. Thus, when it comes to stress and coping there has been extensive extrapolating from work with adults to adolescents. While the literature in this area has grown in the past decade, the evidence to support these conceptualizations is relatively recent. Children and adolescents do experience stress and there are clear manifestations with implications for young people's health and wellbeing. The theory of coping has been readily accepted as a way of understanding how adolescents deal with life circumstances and how they can be helped to deal with these better. The general emphasis with children and adolescence is on building up resilience and developing optimism. Resilience is generally regarded as the ability to recover and move on in the face of difficult or devastating circumstances (Olsson, Bond, Burns, Vella-Brodrick & Sawyer, 2003; Rutter, 1994).

Several attempts have been made to classify stresses as those that are acute, such as a first visit to the dentist, those that are chronic, such as maternal illness, and those that are part of the hassles of daily living, such as having to submit an assignment at school or perform in front of a class (see Compas, 1987). While such classifications maybe helpful for researchers in determining the impact of, for instance, a particular type of chronic event, such as maternal depression on young people's lives[1] groupings have generally not been reliable in predicting how an individual will respond to a particular event.

Definitions of coping

The most frequently cited definition of coping, which has generally been accepted as being relevant across the lifespan, is that of Richard Lazarus. According to Lazarus coping is:

> the cognitive and behavioural efforts to manage specific external or internal demands (and conflicts between them) that are appraised as taxing or exceeding the resources of a person (Lazarus, 1991, 112).

Lazarus' definition of coping emphasizes the context in which the coping actions occur, the attempt rather than the outcome, and the fact that coping is a process that changes over time as the person and the environment are continuously in a dynamic, mutually influential relationship (Lazarus & Folkman, 1984, Folkman & Lazarus 1988). This is generally known as the transactional model of coping.

To date much of the coping research in the child and adolescent area has been predicated on the theorizing of Folkman and Lazarus. However alternate, theory-driven models of coping, such as the multiaxial model of Hobfoll (1998) hold promise for work with young people. Hobfoll's model differs from that of Folkman and Lazarus in that there are six axes which account for the pro-social and antisocial, the active and passive components of coping actions and the direct and indirect dimensions of the response. This model attempts to shift the emphasis from an individualistic to a collectivist perspective. While we teach individuals to develop their coping skills so as to achieve better personal outcomes, the collectivist perspective recognizes that the individual is embedded in a family and other social collectives, which Hobfoll calls 'tribes', that may have both capacity and responsibility to assist in coping. For example, a classroom can be organized to support students, a community can provide food, shelter and recreational opportunities and so on. Thus it is not only the individual who carries the responsibility for optimum outcomes.

Another aspect of Hobfoll's approach is that it emphasizes the notion of individuals' attempts to conserve their resources (COR theory), that is, to maintain that which they value and guard against loss when resources are threatened. Resources in this sense can be material, social or esteem-related. While the model has yet to be tested with children and adolescents, it appears to have validity in that it affirms that individuals wish to hold on to that which they have and acquire that which they value. This seems to hold true for young people as much as adults in that friendships, possessions and pride are valued resources, particularly when they are under threat. A further promise of this model is its relevance for educators in that it includes a notion of values, and those principles and actions that might be included in the teaching of coping skills. Hobfoll's theory also helps us to appreciate that, while we can assist individuals to enhance their coping through the optimum utilization of resources that may be external, such as possessions, or internal, such as coping skills, sometimes the resources that are available to the individual need to be enhanced, such as the compensation for disadvantage.

Another recent development in the coping field has been the notion of proactive coping (Greenglass, 2002; Schwarzer & Taubert, 2002) with its emphasis on goal management. Proactive copers are likely to have goals that they strive to achieve. They often anticipate situations that they are likely to encounter; they are proactive rather than reactive. That is, proactive coping is future-oriented rather than compensating for loss or alleviating harm. Proactive coping is helpful in terms of goal setting and goal getting. Those with goals are likely to be happier in their everyday lives.

So what is coping?

From descriptions by young people of how they cope and using empirical procedures to determine the dimensions of coping Frydenberg and Lewis (1993a) emphasize attempts to achieve a homeostatic balance between people and their environments. Coping is defined as:

> a set of cognitive and affective actions which arise in response to a particular concern. They represent an attempt to restore the equilibrium or to remove the turbulence for the individual. This may be done by solving the problem (that is, removing the stimulus) or accommodating to the concern without bringing about a solution (page 255).

This definition emphasizes that where situations are uncontrollable and when problems are not able to be solved, such as in the situation of chronic illness, the individual accommodates to the situation.

Our coping is made up of our thoughts, feelings and actions in response to the demands of our everyday lives. Psychologists tend to measure many aspects of human behaviour in order to understand what is going on in a given population and also to help people understand their own behaviour in a given circumstance. We measure intelligence (IQ), emotional intelligence (EQ), personality, temperament, achievement in a given field such as reading or mathematics, stress, anxiety, depression and so on. So coping is no exception.

❀ Coping is our way of dealing with our world and the problems that life dishes out
❀ There is no formula for coping and no right or wrong coping because there are different problems and situations and different needs for each person
❀ We need to deal with each problem situation by drawing on a range of coping strategies

Coping is about how we view a situation and choose to respond to it. Do we see a situation as one of threat, harm, loss or challenge? The same situation can be seen as a threat by one person and a challenge by another. A meeting with one's boss, entering a competition or committing to a relationship can each be seen as a challenge by some or approached with trepidation by others. Our *thoughts* affect our *feelings* and our *actions*. If we can make our thinking more positive, then we will feel more positive and we will be able to act in a positive way. Self-talk is another way to describe the thoughts that we have. It is the things that we say to ourselves to explain events or understand things that have happened. Our feelings are controlled by our self-talk, or our thoughts, not only by things that happen.

EVENT → THOUGHT → FEELINGS → ACTIONS

We can deal effectively with circumstances by drawing on our own experiences (what has worked in the past and what has not), looking at the resources we have and calling on others for support. Some coping strategies deal directly with the problem, others may just alleviate the stress for a time but do not lead to a solution. Some strategies work better than others. There are infinite ways of coping but we tend to use a limited range of strategies. We often stick to the same habitual ways of coping. That's great if it works, not so great if it doesn't work. We need to kick bad habits and develop good ones. If we expand our ways of coping, that is, increase our coping repertoire we increase our range of options for coping, leaving us with new possibilities and new ways to deal with problems.

Even when there are situations that we cannot control, such as an illness experienced by ourselves or someone close to us is, there are some strategies that can help us cope more effectively. Sharing the grief with a friend or counsellor or writing about the pain are examples. We are in control. We make the choices about how to deal with circumstances. If we work out what the real problem is, it is easier to choose the most effective strategies. We can choose how to deal with our problems.

Understanding our coping style and having a good look at the way we deal with problems allows us to see both the positive and negative strategies that we tend to use. Once we understand how we cope, then we can concentrate on:

getting into good coping HABITS

and

getting out of bad coping HABITS

Measurement of coping

There are different ways of conceptualizing coping. Families of coping have been proposed by Zimmer-Gembeck & Skinner (2008), including problem-solving, information seeking, helplessness, escape, self-reliance, support seeking, delegation, social isolation, accommodation, negotiation, submission and opposition. These families are made up of coping strategies that function as part of the adaptive process and have related behaviours.

Others have grouped the stress response into voluntary and involuntary which, in turn, when grouped as engagement coping, is made up of primary control coping and secondary control coping (Connor-Smith, Compas, Wadsworth, Thomsen & Saltzman, 2000). While each of the groupings have their value for research and application, we have chosen to empirically identify the coping strategies of young people by asking them to respond to the question, 'What do you do to cope?'

When we are asked to reflect on how we cope and to describe the strategies that we use, we are likely to nominate one, two or three things that readily come to mind. These few strategies that are spontaneously nominated are generally not enough for us to understand the full range of human behaviour. So, in order to get a comprehensive picture of young people's coping skills, we first asked hundreds of adolescents to describe how they cope. In that way we generated some 2,034 descriptions of coping. Not everyone used all these strategies but each of these strategies was reportedly used by some of the people some of the time. It became clear that theoretically there are an infinite number of ways that we cope but there were many strategies that could be grouped together to describe what we do to manage our lives.

So, after many trials, the 2,043 strategies were reduced to 18 areas and, more recently, we have added five more. The 23 areas fall into three broader coping styles namely:

❀*Productive coping*, which is comprised of focusing on solving the problem, working hard to achieve, focusing on the positive, seeking relaxing diversions, physical recreation, accepting one's best efforts, trying to be funny, investing in close friends

❀ *Reference to others* includes seeking social support, social action, seeking spiritual support, seeking professional help

❀ *Non-productive coping* is made up of strategies such as worry, seeking to belong, wishful thinking, tension reduction, not coping, ignoring the problem, self-blame, keeping to self, acting up, getting sick and giving up

It is evident that on some occasions a strategy may be helpful and on other occasions it is not. For example, to worry is generally not helpful but a modicum of worry before a major performance – be it on stage, an examination or an important interview – can enhance effort and subsequent performance. Similarly, declaring that one does not have the strategies to cope may on rare occasions spur a person on to find new resources but in general it is a declaration of helplessness, which is not helpful. The coping strategies are listed and described in Module 1. Since no list of coping captures all the possible strategies that are used by young people, particularly for different problems and in different contexts, it is important to elicit and discuss anything else that the individual is likely to use to cope.

What we know about coping

One of the most consistent findings in terms of coping is that boys and girls do it differently. Boys and girls often need to cope with different situations but also they are likely to choose different strategies. Boys tend to externalize problems and ascribe blame externally, that is, 'the teacher didn't prepare us for the exam' rather than 'I didn't work hard' or to keep problems to themselves. They also use sport as a release, while girls tend to turn to each other (Frydenberg & Lewis, 1993b). There are also age-related differences and cultural differences. While cross-cultural studies report that there are more similarities than differences in how young people in different countries cope, there are nevertheless some differences in the range of coping strategies that are used by young people in different communities. For example, German and Australian young people are more similar in coping, compared to Columbian and Palestinian young people (Frydenberg, Lewis, Kennedy, Ardila, Frindte, & Hannoun, 2003), so the point has to be made that the context *does* make a difference and no assumptions can be made about any group of young people as to how they should cope. It is what works for them and whether they want to change what they are doing that is the important consideration.

Achievement

When it comes to educational achievement and coping we found in a study of 374 boys in Grades 9, 10 and 11 at an independent boys' school in Melbourne, Australia (Parsons, Frydenberg & Poole, 1996) that, when the 'capable' boys were compared with the regular student body of males, that the former were less likely to declare that they did not have the strategies to cope than were the latter. This indicates that the 'capable' students perceive themselves as coping satisfactorily. When the link between achievement, ability and coping was considered, it was found that boys who achieved better than would be expected on the basis of ability alone (known as 'over-achievement') utilized more social support as a strategy for coping. Social support is generally used more by girls than by boys but it would seem that boys may benefit from these strategies. In a comparable study of girls (Noto, 1995) academic achievement was also linked to the use of social support as well as working hard, solving the problem and being positive. In contrast, less academic achievement was linked to a declaration of not having the strategies to cope, that is, using tension reduction and ignoring the problem. It was found that too many attempts to fit in with friends had negative consequences on achievement. Thus teaching young people to use more productive coping strategies and fewer non-productive ones may help to increase academic achievement.

Wellbeing and coping

The relationship between wellbeing and coping is an important one since wellbeing is not only the absence of illness but an index of health and satisfaction with life. These, in turn, can impact how an individual copes and, in turn, good coping can also impact health and wellbeing. It was clearly established in a study of 1,264 12–16-year-old secondary school students (Frydenberg & Lewis, 2002) that there is a strong association between coping strategies described as non-productive and a dysfunctional state of being. For example, young people who use more self-blame are in a significantly more dysfunctional state of being than those who use less, and those who use less experienced better wellbeing. These findings gave us a clear signal that preventive interventions should focus on the reduction of maladaptive coping strategies rather than on just the more common goal of increasing productive coping skills, such as problem-focused coping, and, in particular, should tackle the overuse of self-blame.

In another study, where we explored the relationship between wellbeing, coping and school connectedness, 536 (241 boys and 295 girls) Year 8 students responded to an in-class survey and the Adolescent Coping Scale as part of a larger study (Frydenberg, Care, Freeman & Chan, in press). It was found that a productive coping style was positively related both to a reported sense of wellbeing and to a lesser extent to school connectedness.

A non-productive coping style was found to be inversely related to students' sense of wellbeing and connection to school. Students' sense of emotional wellbeing was positively associated with school connectedness. The negative relationship between non-productive coping and emotional wellbeing and, to a lesser extent, with school connectedness highlighted the importance of taking into account the influence of risk factors as well as positive factors when focusing on enhancement of wellbeing and connectedness in secondary school students. That is, reducing the use of non-productive coping could reduce the risk of poor wellbeing and poor engagement with school. Overall there is a critical connection between levels of student engagement, emotional wellbeing and styles of coping. That is, young people who are less engaged tended to utilize fewer problem-solving skills and tended to rely more on the use of non-productive strategies.

Dysfunctional behaviour and coping

There is an accumulating body of evidence that various forms of behaviour that could be characterized as dysfunctional are associated with greater utilization of non-productive coping responses and lesser use of productive ones.

In a study by Chesire and Campbell (1997) the coping of 30 learning-disabled students (aged 13–15 years) found that, compared to average achieving adolescents, the learning disabled group used more wishful thinking and tended to believe that they were not coping. Further, learning-disabled students used less productive strategies such as focusing on the positive, relaxing and working to solve the problem. Learning-disabled students were much less likely to employ coping strategies that focused on the problem than their average achieving peers.

A second study (McTaggart, 1996) compared the coping strategies of eight students (six male and two female) attending a special post-primary teaching unit for behaviourally disordered students to the coping strategies used by 24 peers (14 male and 18 female) drawn from Year 8 classes in two mainstream settings. The students in the teaching unit were considered to be at risk of exclusion from high school since they had been suspended for more than ten days within the previous six months or within the current school year. The mainstream groups were characterized by greater use of solve the problem which, in conjunction with more use of work hard, represented a powerful combination of approach (solution-focused) coping. Strategies more closely associated with membership of the teaching unit group were keep to self, seek professional help and social action. These data indicate that membership within the mainstream group was clearly associated with use of effective, problem-focused coping strategies. However, differences between groups in non-productive coping were not as apparent.

Implications

Appraisal is an important first step in the coping process. In recognition of the critical part that it is seen to play, any programme that attempts to develop young people's coping skills through the development of positive cognitions also needs to teach skills of positive cognitive appraisal.

Measurement also plays a major part in advancing theoretical understanding of the coping process in describing population trends, providing guidelines for educational programming and facilitating clinical interventions. In this largely cognitive process, self-awareness, which can be raised through individuals examining their own coping profiles – that is, what strategies they use a lot and what they use a little – and choosing to engage in self-directed behavioural change. That is, an individual may choose to change the strategies that are not productive in particular encounters and expand coping repertoires as a resource for the future. Changing from 'stress talk' to 'health talk', and changing 'stress company' to 'helping company' are important in changing to a positive mood set and, as such, they are useful precursors to developing positive cognitions. Each in their way contributes to adaptive coping. Working or spending leisure time with a group of peers who are engaged in health talk promotes the use of productive coping strategies and reduces the likelihood of using non-productive ones, enabling skills to be built in a climate of optimism.

There are some indications from the research on stresses that do not auger well for young people as they traverse through adolescence. It should be possible to avert some of the difficulties in dealing with life circumstances through enhancing an understanding of coping and through the development of coping strategies. While there is no inherently right or wrong coping strategy, it is important that both children and adults learn to judge circumstances appropriately as being within their own ambit of control and within their range of adaptive coping resources. Young people can learn to expand their coping repertoires to use more of the available strategies in particular contexts.

In general, when it comes to adjustment, both males and females who exhibit optimum adjustment are those who report dealing with tension with a high proportion of salutary effort; that is, those who utilize mature coping as opposed to stress release, so it is the broadening of positive coping strategies that is being proposed.

Longitudinal studies indicate that, in order to avert the development of non-productive strategies, we need to consider both the sex and the age of the person for whom the programme is being developed. For example, there appear to be indications that it is useful to intervene in the psychosocial development of adolescents of 14–16 years of age in order to attract their interest and commitment and to capitalize on the particular developmental stage that they are traversing (Frydenberg & Lewis, 2000). Teaching coping at this age or even earlier is recommended because the greatest shift in coping occurs during these years. This would appear to be the optimum time to engage the adolescents in reflection upon their coping behaviour and in discussion about the benefits of using particular strategies. Such an approach would appear to be particularly relevant for girls, who not only exhibit a greater shift in coping than do boys during the ages of 12–16, but whose ability to cope decreases significantly during this period. The fact that boys and girls develop differently in their patterns of coping with age has implications for the timing and content of coping skills development programmes.

In order to foster healthy social and emotional development we need to change the language of despair to a language of optimism and ability. Talking about coping is a step in the right direction. How people think to a large extent determines how they feel. A greater capacity to reflect on their situation and to assess the appropriate responses for them would help. If there is an emphasis on language and thinking to reflect capabilities (coping) rather than despair (stress) then it is likely to bring about a change in how people feel about themselves. Such a shift will contribute to the optimal development of young people. This is very much the business of education.

Learning to cope

What the recent movements in psychology have shown us is that it is possible to learn new ways of appraising and responding to situations. A positive mindset is an asset, but having a resource pool of situational, interpersonal and personal resources is all important. A belief in one's capacities to cope is achieved through an appreciation that there are skills that can be learned. These skills not only help us to survive but also assist us to thrive. The conceptual areas of coping have led to the development of structured coping skills programmes that have been demonstrated to be of benefit to both the instructor and the student or client. When the programme is taught in a universal setting, that is to a whole class or group, it is those who are in the greatest need who benefit the most. When the programme is taught to a special group, for example, those who have experienced grief and loss, a learning-disabled group of young people or those young people in need of social skills, there are benefits for the whole group. These adaptations are discussed in Section 3, which details some of these tailored approaches to teaching coping.

We know it is possible to teach coping skills. Often the programmes are scripted, much as the one in this book, but the instructors adapt the scripts to meet the population needs. We know from numerous implementations of similar programmes to the one presented here that students learn to cope better and learn to reduce non-productive coping strategies. We have found the same results in single-sex school settings as in co-educational settings and found similar outcomes in the early years and in the later years of high school. In a recent study of students in a rural setting, where teachers implemented a programme of coping skills to a whole class group, those students who were at high risk for developing depression showed substantial decrease in their use of unhelpful coping strategies, particularly use of self-blaming. Encouragingly, they continued to decrease their reliance on these unhelpful strategies over the subsequent 12-month period. Students then received a booster intervention using the CD-ROM *Coping for Success* (Frydenberg, 2007). Following this programme, students reported significant increases in use of productive coping strategies that involved gaining support and referring to others. The use of the booster programme was successful in facilitating increased use of helpful coping responses and enabled students to review and reflect on their coping.

How the 12 modules can be used

All the evidence leads to us to believe that coping skills can be developed. Each of the 12 modules has been trialled and evaluated in various formats with various populations and the results are promising (Frydenberg 2008, Frydenberg, Eacott & Clark, 2008). The most recent was the evaluation of Module 10 (Coping in cyberworld) (Lam, 2008).

In one study, in which a teacher implemented 10 modules of a coping skills programme, the teacher monitored her own coping skills development as she taught the programme to her students and she reported the changes both in her students and herself (Huxley, Freedman & Frydenberg, 2007).

Several of the early modules, such as those relating to the language of coping and the use of non-productive coping strategies, may be extended and taught over a longer period, that is, over longer than one session. The first eight modules are best taught sequentially over an extended period rather than as a coping intensive. Both formats have been tried but better outcomes are achieved when the students have opportunities to rehearse between sessions.

While all the modules are suitable for 12–18 years olds, the final four modules are considered in some settings to be most relevant in the latter years of secondary school, where the main interest might be for students to set goals and managing time effectively when it comes to studies. Although the modules have been designed to be offered to groups of students, the activities can be adapted to both small and large groups. It is possible to adapt the activities and develop a completely individualized programme that is particularly suitable for clinical or counselling interventions. Additionally there are individualized activities that can be used as homework. (See also pages 5–6.)

As we have demonstrated in our research, maintenance of skills is a problem. Students can be provided with the CD-ROM *Coping for Success* (Frydenberg & Lewis, 2007) as a personalized resource or it can be used as a booster programme. It is readily available from the Australian Council for Educational Research and also through its international distributors.

Evaluation

Evaluation of any programme of instruction is highly desirable. The quizzes can be used as an informal evaluation, as can qualitative statements about what individuals have learned and what they now do differently.

Additionally, in all our research studies we have used the Adolescent Coping Scale (Frydenberg & Lewis, 1993a) as pre- and post-measures since the instrument itself teaches and reinforces the language of coping. It provides a profile chart that an individual can use to reflect on their 'before' and 'after' completion of the programme of coping. It is also an efficient tool that provides quantitative data. These assessments are done by a psychologist or someone trained in psychometrics.

Where it is not possible to use the instrument then the instructor can devise a grid with the 23 coping areas and ask the participants to plot what they use a lot, a little and not at all before and after the programme.

Notes

1 For example, there is a greater likelihood of young people experiencing depression following maternal depression

SECTION 2

The modules of the programme

Module 1 – The language of coping

'Learning to cope is helpful so you can handle different challenges
that life throws at you.'

Mike, 17

Contents

Group and classwork activities
Individual instruction and homework activities
Resources

Learning outcomes

The module aims to introduce the concept of coping, explore individual styles, and facilitate an understanding of the various coping strategies. By the end of this module students will be able to identify the difference between productive and non-productive coping and the frequency with which particular strategies are used.

In this module students will:

✿ Be exposed to the language of coping
✿ Describe what coping strategies they currently use and how these may be improved
✿ Listen to or reflect on the coping experiences of others

Instructor's notes

For most young people, adolescence is a time marked by biological maturation, relationship changes, the development of identity and increased independence. Some make these transitions smoothly but, for others, this period creates confusion, anxiety, conflict and uncertainty. The strength to cope with these challenges is drawn from previous adjustments, family support and self-motivation. Coping during adolescence can be conceptualized as adaptive functioning; that is, the way young people interact with their environment and adapt to stressful events. A capacity to adapt so as to achieve the best outcomes for the individual is also fundamental to the art of coping. The philosophy that underpins the coping skills programme is that we can all do what we do better. An analogy can be made with sporting endeavours, where an individual strives to achieve his or her best performance and often it is a personal best rather than a competitive one.

While it is normal to experience worries and concerns as a part of the maturation process, for some young people these feelings can escalate into a stress. This can have serious consequences when combined with a deficit in coping resources. Depression, anxiety and suicide are just some of the negative sequelae significantly increasing in adolescent populations.

The aim of this module is to provide young people with a coping vernacular that allows them to build a foundation from which they may implement change and improve their coping strategies. The cognitive behavioural approach which underpins this programme relies heavily on using a consistent language to describe productive and non-productive coping strategies. The terms that will be introduced in this module will appear throughout the manual. This terminology is the product of many years of empirical research and professional practice in the field of adolescent wellbeing.

Setting the context

The following activities are designed to help students think about the way they currently cope and to introduce them to the *language of coping*. They facilitate self-reflection and discussion. In order to create an environment where young people feel comfortable enough to share, it is important to find a quiet and private space. If you are conducting a group or class activity it is important to inform students that all information shared within the group will remain confidential (unless there are any overriding safety or legal concerns). All members of the group should be discouraged from repeating any information about another student outside of the group.

Note: it is advisable for students to have a ring binder so that they can keep their work organized as they complete the activities.

Group and classwork activities

Ice breaker: Introductions

Time: 10 minutes

Materials: None

Instructions: Instruct the group to sit in a circle. The purpose of this activity is to help students become better acquainted with one another. While students may already know each other's names, they sometimes know few personal details about the other members of the cohort. Begin the session by having students sit alongside someone with whom they would not ordinarily sit. Once all students are seated, ask them to form pairs with the person sitting next to them. Working in pairs, allow the students 5 minutes to establish:

1. The other person's name
2. One thing the other person is really good at
3. One thing the other person would like to know about coping

Once 5 minutes have elapsed, ask the pairs to introduce one another to the group and share with the group the things they discovered about the person.

Activity 1: Coping brainstorm

Time: 25 minutes

Materials: Whiteboard, coloured whiteboard markers (red, black and green)

Instructions: To encourage students' willingness to share information, inform the group that they will not be individually called upon to disclose personal information. Let them know that the function of this exercise is to explore how young people cope generally. Using the whiteboard and black whiteboard marker, ask the students to brainstorm as many words as possible that might describe how one might cope with a stressful event.

You might like to use the following list of coping strategies to prompt responses. The first 18 coping strategies have been found to be the most commonly reported by adolescents and utilized in much of the coping research from which this programme has been developed; the final five in the list also occur regularly and have been added more recently.

Seek social support
Focus on solving the problem
Work hard and achieve
Worry
Invest in close friends
Seek to belong

Wishful thinking

Social action

Tension reduction

Not coping

Ignore the problem

Self-blame

Keep to self

Seek spiritual support

Focus on the positive

Seek professional help

Seek relaxing diversions

Physical recreation

Accept my best efforts

Act up

Get sick

Give up

Try to be funny

Teaching tip

As the students are brainstorming coping words, it could be useful to use some of the terms listed so that students are incidentally exposed to the language that will be explored in greater detail in future modules.

Once a substantial volume of words has been collected, the next step is to help the students identify which coping strategies are productive and which are not. The list might look like this:

Productive coping strategies	**Non-productive coping strategies**
Seek social support	Worry
Focus on solving the problem	Seek to belong
Work hard and achieve	Wishful thinking
Invest in close friends	Tension reduction
Social action	Not coping
Seek spiritual support	Ignore the problem
Focus on the positive	Self-blame
Seek professional help	Keep to self
Seek relaxing diversions	Get sick
Physical recreation	Give up
Accept my best efforts	Act up
Try to be funny	

As the productive and non-productive coping words are identified, circle the productive coping strategies in green and circle the non-productive coping strategies in red. Place a line under the strategies that involve a third party. Explain to the students that there are three categories of coping:

1. Productive
2. Non-productive
3. Reference to others

While *reference to others* strategies are generally productive and thus a subset of the *productive* group (strategies such as professional help, seek spiritual support, invest in close friends and seek social support, try to be funny), they are important in their own right as much successful adaptation is reliant on helpful relationships and working well with others.

What coping strategies do you use?

Provide the students with 3 minutes to discuss with a partner which coping strategies they use *a lot*. Once this has been completed, provide the students with an additional 3 minutes to discuss which coping strategies they use *very little*.

To finish this activity it is recommended that students be provided with access to external resources should they have significant worries or concerns. It is suggested that the students are given the contact details of their school counsellor, school chaplain and some 24-hour anonymous telephone counselling contacts relevant to their area.

Activity 2: Coping capers

Time: 25 minutes

Materials: Two sets of Coping Cards (see page 39) and a stop watch

Instructions: The function of this activity is to provide young people with an interactive way in which they can be exposed to some of the terminology that will be used throughout the programme. Photocopy the Coping Cards on page 39; you will need two sets of these. As this resource can be used again, you might find it useful to laminate the cards prior to distributing them. Once the Coping Cards have been prepared, make sure they are well mixed up. There are 23 Coping Card pairs, which would ideally suit a group of 23 students. This is not essential and the activity can be adapted to any size group. Each of the coping cards represents one of the 23 coping strategies discussed in Activity 1. If you have a smaller number of students, you may decide to use fewer Coping Card pairs. If you have a larger group, it might be useful to create student teams of two to three individuals.

Allocate each student a Coping Card. Explain to them that you are going to time how long it takes them to match each of the Coping Cards with their respective identical pair. The only rule for this game is that they must find the Coping Card pair in silence. They may use sign language, gestures or non-verbal cues, but talking or whispering are not allowed. Using the stop watch, time students and record how long the activity takes to complete.

Once students have matched the Coping Card pairs, you might like to review the activity with the group. What worked well and what didn't? How long did the activity take? You could perhaps pose the question: 'What could be improved if the activity were to be repeated?' Some responses might be:

- More non-verbal communication
- Approaching each individual member calmly
- Asking fellow students to hold out their Coping Card
- No talking
- Keeping calm and cool

Run the activity again as above. Again, using the stop watch, time how long it takes them to match the Coping Cards. Ask the group to sit in a circle in the newly formed pairs. Use the following list of prompt questions to initiate discussion:

- Did the group perform faster during time trial one or time trial two?
- What attributes did we use on the more successful time trial?
- Sometimes when we are timed with a stop watch, it can make us feel tense or anxious. When feeling this way, what strategies did people use to remain in control so as to complete the activity as successfully as possible?

Ask each pair to read out their Coping Card title. As each coping strategy is read out, ask the group:

- Do you think this is a productive or non-productive coping strategy?
- Is this a strategy that requires another person (i.e., reference to others)?
- What does this coping strategy mean for you?

Activity 3: Coping charades
Time: 15 minutes

Materials: Coping Cards (see page 39)

Instructions: Place the Coping Cards in a large box. Similar to the game of charades, students take turns to pull out a card, keeping it hidden from the other members of the group. Without talking, each student is required to act out the respective Coping Card strategy they have chosen, while the other group members attempt to guess what is being portrayed.

Teaching tip
This game works best if the students are seated in a large circle. You may allow some time for discussion to take place after each turn.

It is important to reinforce that, while there are a variety of different coping strategies that young people may use when faced with a difficulty, coping strategies can be used differently by individuals depending on the context and the unique needs of the individual.

Reflection

Time: 10 minutes

Ask students to imagine themselves engaging in one productive coping strategy discussed in the session that they do not frequently use; a coping strategy that they think could be improved. Give them an additional 3 minutes to reflect on this and share their thoughts.

Close the session by providing the group with the tipsheet entitled Hot Tip Number 1: Coping found on page 44. The tipsheet provides a summary of the coping terminology used in the above activities. This resource may be photocopied and handed to students to reflect upon at a later date.

Individual instruction and homework activities

This section lists activities that students can complete independently or in one-on-one instruction. These activities may also be used as homework to consolidate concepts covered in group or class work activities. The pages are designed to be reproduced and may be collected and kept by students in a workbook-type format.

Prior to beginning the following activities, provide each young person with the tipsheet Hot Tip Number 1: Coping found on page 44, if you have not already done so. Allow sufficient time for this to be read and discussed.

Activity 1.1: Coping strategies

List the three main worries or concerns that might be experienced by someone of your age.

1.

_____

2.

_____

3.

_____

A. There are 18 main coping strategies plus five more that commonly occur. These 23 strategies fall into one of three categories: productive, non-productive and reference to others (that is, involving somebody else). From the 23 different coping strategies below select three strategies that you *commonly* use to deal with your problems.

PRODUCTIVE	**NON-PRODUCTIVE**	**REFERENCE TO OTHERS**
☐ Focus on solving the problem	☐ Not coping	☐ Invest in close friends
☐ Work hard and achieve	☐ Worry	☐ Seek social support
☐ Focus on the positive	☐ Ignore the problem	☐ Seek professional help
☐ Seek relaxing diversions	☐ Wishful thinking	☐ Try to be funny
☐ Physical recreation	☐ Tension reduction	☐ Seek spiritual support
☐ Accept my best efforts	☐ Self-blame	☐ Seek to belong
	☐ Get sick	☐ Social action
	☐ Give up	
	☐ Keep to self	
	☐ Act up	

For each of the three strategies, write down whether it helps you or does not help you to solve your problems. Additionally, consider how it helps you and why it does not help you to solve the problem.

1.

_____

2.

_____

3.

_____

B. From the 23 different coping strategies below select three strategies that you *hardly ever* use to solve your problems.

PRODUCTIVE	NON-PRODUCTIVE	REFERENCE TO OTHERS
☐ Focus on solving the problem	☐ Not coping	☐ Invest in close friends
☐ Work hard and achieve	☐ Worry	☐ Seek social support
☐ Focus on the positive	☐ Ignore the problem	☐ Seek professional help
☐ Seek relaxing diversions	☐ Wishful thinking	☐ Try to be funny
☐ Physical recreation	☐ Tension reduction	☐ Seek spiritual support
☐ Accept my best efforts	☐ Self-blame	☐ Seek to belong
	☐ Get sick	☐ Social action
	☐ Give up	
	☐ Keep to self	
	☐ Act up	

For each strategy, write down whether or not it would help you to solve your problems and why.

1.
_____

2.
_____

3.
_____

C. Of the 23 strategies, which strategies would you like to use more? Write down your reasons why.

PRODUCTIVE	NON-PRODUCTIVE	REFERENCE TO OTHERS
☐ Focus on solving the problem	☐ Not coping	☐ Invest in close friends
☐ Work hard and achieve	☐ Worry	☐ Seek social support
☐ Focus on the positive	☐ Ignore the problem	☐ Seek professional help
☐ Seek relaxing diversions	☐ Wishful thinking	☐ Try to be funny
☐ Physical recreation	☐ Tension reduction	☐ Seek spiritual support
☐ Accept my best efforts	☐ Self-blame	☐ Seek to belong
	☐ Get sick	☐ Social action
	☐ Give up	
	☐ Keep to self	
	☐ Act up	

1.
_____

2.
_____

3.

Activity 1.2: Coping with different situations

A. Read the following situation:

Situation: Jess: 'I am having a party on Friday night. I feel really nervous. I have never had a party before and I am worried that no one will turn up.'

What coping strategy or strategies could Jess use?

_____

What could the outcome be of using this strategy or these strategies?

_____

B. Read the following situation:

Situation: Jenna: 'I have found the best dress to wear to the formal dance at the weekend. Mum says she won't buy it for me because it is too short.'

What coping strategy or strategies could Jenna use?

_____

What could the outcome be of using this strategy or these strategies?

_____

C. Read the following situation:

Situation: Josh has tried really hard to get his driver's licence, but has failed the test three times. Josh says 'he can't be bothered studying', but he feels jealous of all his mates because they have got their licence.

What coping strategy or strategies could Josh use?

_____

What could the outcome be of using this strategy or these strategies?

D. Describe three different situations that you have had to deal with in the past, e.g. doing your homework or going out with friends, deciding which friends to invite to your birthday. Choose a coping strategy that you could have used, or did use, to deal with each situation.

Describe the first situation:

_____

What coping strategy could you use?

_____

What could the outcome be of using this strategy?

_____

Describe the second situation:

_____

What coping strategy could you use?

_____

What could the outcome be of using this strategy?

_____

Activity 1.2: Coping with different situations – continued

Describe the third situation:

_____

What coping strategy could you use?

_____

What could the outcome be of using this strategy?

_____

E. What do you think of the outcomes? Would you deal with the situations in the same way again?

_____

Activity 1.3: Coping styles

Consider the 23 coping strategies:

PRODUCTIVE	**NON-PRODUCTIVE**	**REFERENCE TO OTHERS**
☐ Focus on solving the problem	☐ Not coping	☐ Invest in close friends
☐ Work hard and achieve	☐ Worry	☐ Seek social support
☐ Focus on the positive	☐ Ignore the problem	☐ Seek professional help
☐ Seek relaxing diversions	☐ Wishful thinking	☐ Try to be funny
☐ Physical recreation	☐ Tension reduction	☐ Seek spiritual support
☐ Accept my best efforts	☐ Self-blame	☐ Seek to belong
	☐ Get sick	☐ Social action
	☐ Give up	
	☐ Keep to self	
	☐ Act up	

A. Think of a situation in which you have used solving the problem coping (productive coping).

B. Think of a situation in which you have used the help of others (reference to others).

C. Think of a situation in which you have used a strategy which was unhelpful or negative in dealing with the problem (non-productive coping).

D. Do you think that you tend to use one particular coping style more than the others?

E. Which coping style would you like to use more often?

F. Which coping style would you like to use less?

Modifying the activities for students with additional needs

You might like to use the Coping Cards below to play additional card games such as Memory, Concentration or Snap. The rules for how to play this game are on page 46. These games would be ideally suited to students with additional learning needs or they could be used as an extended activity. These traditional card games are easy to play and generally already understood by most students. These games are repetitive and are ideal for exposing students to the coping terminology used in this manual.

Resources
Coping cards

You will need to make two copies of the following cards. Photocopy the cards onto heavyweight bond paper. Cut the cards out and laminate them, so that they may be used again.

SELF-BLAME

KEEP TO SELF

GET SICK

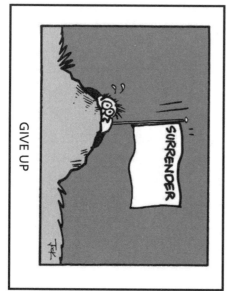

GIVE UP

SEEK SOCIAL SUPPORT

PHYSICAL RECREATION

TENSION REDUCTION

NOT COPE

SEEK SPIRITUAL SUPPORT

SEEK PROFESSIONAL HELP

INVEST IN CLOSE FRIENDS

TRY TO BE FUNNY

WISHFUL THINKING

FOCUS ON SOLVING THE PROBLEM

WORRY

WORK HARD AND ACHIEVE

IGNORE THE PROBLEM

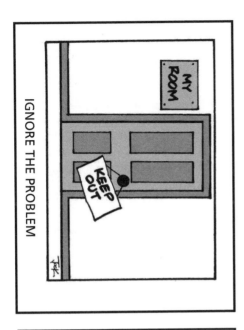

SEEK TO BELONG

FOCUS ON THE POSITIVE

SOCIAL ACTION

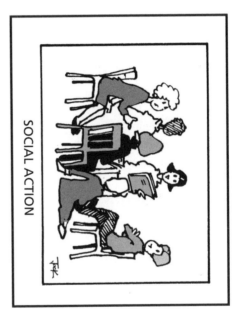

SEEK RELAXING DIVERSIONS

Tipsheet: Hot tip number 1: coping

Coping is how we *view* a situation and how we choose to *respond* to it. We need to cope with situations in all areas of our lives – *home*, *school* and the *community*. We can use different coping strategies in different situations and with different people.

There are many ways (including actions, thoughts and feelings) that people use to manage their problems or concerns. There are many different ways of coping and 23 main strategies have been identified:

1. **Seek social support**
   Sharing the problem with friends or relatives so they can listen and/or help you to deal with it.

2. **Focus on solving the problem**
   Tackling the problem by learning about it and taking into account different points of view or options.

3. **Work hard and achieve**
   Applying yourself and putting in all your efforts to succeed.

4. **Worry**
   Being concerned about the future.

5. **Invest in close friends**
   Relying on a close friend or relationship.

6. **Seek to belong**
   Caring or being concerned about what others think; wanting to be accepted.

7. **Wishful thinking**
   Hoping that things will turn out well.

8. **Social action**
   Letting others know about the concern and getting support by writing petitions or organizing a meeting.

9. **Tension reduction**
   Trying to make yourself feel better by doing something to release tension, such as eating or drinking too much.

10. **Not coping**
    Not doing anything that helps deal with the problem.

11. **Ignore the problem**
    Trying to block out the problem.

12. **Self-blame**
    When you see yourself as responsible for the problem or worry.

13. **Keep to self**
    Withdrawing from others and trying to keep them
    from knowing about your concerns.

14. **Seek spiritual support**
    Praying and/or believing in assistance from God or a
    spiritual leader.

15. **Focus on the positive**
    Having a cheerful or positive outlook about the
    situation.

16. **Seek professional help**
    Going to a qualified person for help, like a teacher or
    counsellor.

17. **Seek relaxing diversions**
    Doing things to relax (other than sport), such as
    reading, painting or listening to music.

18. **Physical recreation**
    Playing sport, keeping fit.

19. **Accept best efforts**
    Accept how things are because I have done my best.

20. **Acting up**
    Act up and make life difficult for those around me.

21. **Getting sick**
    I just get sick.

22. **Giving up**
    I just give up.

23. **Trying to be funny**
    Try to be funny.

We all cope in different ways and generally tend to use some coping strategies more than others. The 23 strategies can be grouped in three basic styles of coping:

Style 1: Solving the problem
This style includes strategies which work on solving a problem while remaining optimistic, fit, relaxed and socially connected.

Style 2: Non-productive coping
This style includes strategies that are largely negative and avoid the problem.

Style 3: Reference to others
This style includes strategies in which people turn to others for help.
You can face the challenges that come your way with the knowledge that you CAN COPE!

Rules for playing the games

Memory or Concentration

Spread a set of coping cards face-down on a flat surface. Each player takes turns in flipping two cards over. If the two cards form a pair, the player collects the pair. If the two cards do not form a pair they are returned to their original location on the flat surface. This process is repeated until all cards have been matched in pairs. The player who has the most pairs once all cards have gone is the winner.

Snap

Split the deck of coping cards evenly among players. Each player ensures that their set of cards is face-down. Each player, in turn, picks up one card from their own deck and places the card face-up in the centre. Players continue to take turns to reveal one card at a time until a pair is found. The player who first sees the pair puts their hand on the pile of cards and calls 'Snap!', and gets to keep the pair as well as the pile of cards. The player who ends up with the biggest pile of cards is the winner.

Coping quiz

1. Identify three productive coping strategies.

2. Identify three non-productive coping strategies.

3. Identify two strategies that you would consider to involve somebody else (that is, reference to others).

Further reading

Further readings are generally for the instructor but *Coping for Capable Kids* was written for teachers, students and parents, so students could be alerted to its availability.

Cohen, L. & E. Frydenberg. (1993), *Coping for Capable Kids*. Melbourne: Hawker Brownlow.

Cohen, L., & Frydenberg, E. (1995), *Coping for Capable Kids*. Waco: Prufrock Press.

Frydenberg, E. (2008), *Adolescent Coping: Advances in Theory Research and Practice*. London: Routledge.

Frydenberg, E. (2007), *Coping for Success*, CD-ROM, Melbourne: Australian Council for Educational Research.

Module 2 – Positive thinking

'I cope with things by focusing on something positive, breathing and listening to music to unwind.'

Steph, 15

Contents

Learning outcomes

The aim of this module is to facilitate an awareness of the connection between thoughts and feelings and to introduce basic skills in thought evaluation and reframing. By the end of this module students will have a general understanding of the role of thoughts on feelings and behaviour.

In this session students will:

❀ Identify and describe positive and negative thinking related to coping

❧ Evaluate thinking and its influence on feelings and behaviour

❧ Generate more helpful thoughts to replace negative thoughts in times when faced with a difficulty

Instructor's notes

The use of positive thinking as a coping strategy in this programme is underpinned by Cognitive Behaviour Therapy (CBT), a psychological approach concerned with identifying the role of cognitions (our thoughts) in relation to effect (how we feel) and behaviour (what we do); that is, the understanding that faulty cognitions are responsible for maladaptive behaviour and unpleasant emotional states (Faust & Katchen, 2004; Stallard, 2002). CBT is an empirically validated approach that has been used successfully with a variety of treatment populations including children who have suffered sexual abuse (Cohen & Mannarino, 1998), Post-traumatic Stress Disorder (Cohen, Deblinger & Mannarino, 2004; Faust & Katchen, 2004; King, Tonge, Mullen, Myerson, Heyne, Rollings & Ollendick, 2000; Smith, Perin & Yule, 1999), Generalized Anxiety Disorder (Kendall, 2000) and depression (Lewinsohn & Clarke, 1999).

Positive thinking is an essential tool for coping. Young people who lack positive thinking skills tend to blame others for their misfortunes, compare themselves negatively to their peers, be impulsive and have poor self-esteem. Adolescents who are able to critically evaluate their thoughts and think positively are better equipped to cope and to deal with difficult situations. The aim of this module is to provide young people with a general understanding of the importance of positive thinking and how they can apply it to their day to day coping.

Setting the context

This module will allow students to explore many real-life examples of negative thinking, including thoughts they encounter in their day to day lives. To set the context of this session, it is useful to review Module 1 and reinforce the points that there are many ways in which young people cope and some strategies are more productive than others. If working in a class or group, it may also be important to reiterate the importance of confidentiality so that students can feel more comfortable sharing their thoughts.

Another important element in setting the context is the instructor. The instructor provides an invaluable model for positive thinking. Modelling a positive attitude and positive thinking within the group will help consolidate the topics discussed and reinforce the value of adopting a positive attitude.

Group and classwork activities

Ice breaker: Positive thinking ball

Time: 10 minutes

Materials: Ball (or balloon) and felt-tip pen

Instructions: This ice breaker requires a small amount of preparation. You will need a ball (preferably one that can be purchased inexpensively) or a balloon. Using the felt-tip pen, divide the ball into sections so that there is room to write some of the following questions/statements:

- Share with the group one thing you are good at.
- What is your favourite food?
- What is the funniest movie you have seen?
- Tell the group one way you have helped someone. How did it make you feel?
- Tell the group one thing you like about yourself.
- What is your favourite part about coming to school?
- What is one thing you love to do outside of school?
- What is one thing you love to do at school?
- Do you have any pets?
- What is your favourite physical exercise?

This list of questions and statements is not prescriptive and may be modified to suit the needs and age of the group members.

Ask the group to form a circle and throw the ball to each other in a random order. When students catch the ball, they must read out the statement or question closest to the thumb on their right hand and answer it before passing the ball to another student.

Activity 1: Positive power

Time: 30 minutes

Materials: Each student will need a piece of paper and a pen. Use the handout titled Common Thought Distortions (see page 60).

Instructions: Inform the students that they will need to think back to the last assessment they did at school. This may have been a test, an oral presentation or an exam. Once they have a clear picture in their head about this task, ask them to jot down as fast as they can two negative things about their performance on this assessment task. Provide students with approximately 1–2 minutes to do this. To enhance students' willingness to share information, inform the group that they will not be individually called upon to disclose their responses during this activity. Once this is completed, ask students to write down two positive things about how they approached the task. Again, provide 1–2 minutes, taking note of how quickly they are jotting down answers.

Teaching tip

Depending on the student group, this activity can be modified to incorporate positive and negative thoughts about other areas of the students' life. Other examples could include body image, social situations, getting along with peers, or a time when they felt anxious or nervous. If the group you are working with isn't especially studious, then it might be appropriate to choose a different topic.

The next part of this activity involves discussion. Ask your group the following questions:

❀ You have just written something positive about yourself and something negative. Which was the easier to do?

❀ Which did you find you were able to write down faster?

You might like to comment on observations you had regarding how students approached the task. Which of the thought exercises did they finish more quickly?

The final component of the exercise involves an explanation of the activity they have just completed. You might like to use the following script to assist with this:

It is generally thought that most people find it easier to think negative, rather than positive, things about themselves. Our brains tend to reach automatic conclusions about events or situations. Sometimes these thoughts are made without having all the evidence available and are thus not an accurate reflection of the situation. Some people like to think of this as 'our brains being lazy'. It is easier to think negatively, rather than look at the situation critically. This impulsive side to our thinking certainly has its uses. Situations often arise when we need to make quick decisions, such as emergencies. If there is a fire, for example, automatic thoughts are essential for our safety; we need to remove ourselves from the harmful situation. In our day to day life, however, automatic thoughts are not always the best response to a particular situation, especially if we have developed a negative thinking pattern. We can become habitual in our thinking and develop patterns of thought which lead to stress, anxiety and depression. The good news is that we can change our thinking! The first step to overcome negative thinking is to be aware of common thought distortions so that we are better able to challenge our negative thoughts and reframe them in a positive way!

 Provide students with the handout Common Thought Distortions from page 60. Read through this list together and generate examples for each distortion from the students' own experiences.

Activity 2: Thinking about thinking

Time: 15 minutes

Materials: Scenario Cards (see page 59), Common Thought Distortions (see page 60) and the Emotion Meter (see page 61).

Instructions: There are two main sections to this activity: Thought Brainstorm and Thought Evaluation.

A. Thought brainstorm

The aim of this section of the activity is to generate as many thoughts as possible for any given scenario. Students should be made aware that there are no right or wrong answers. The goal of this activity is to demonstrate that there can be an endless number of thought responses to any one event. It also demonstrates how the perceptions, beliefs and thoughts of individuals differ. Using the Scenario Cards on page 59, ask students in the group to take a card at random from the pile and read out the scenario on it. Once this has been done, ask the group to brainstorm as many responses as they can to a given scenario.

For example:

Student: 'Scenario 1: Your teacher tells you that today you will be doing a pop quiz without any warning.'

Instructor: 'What are some of the thoughts you might have upon finding out this news?'

Group brainstorm ideas: 'I am going to fail', 'That's unfair', 'We shouldn't have to put up with this', 'She is so mean', 'I hate this school', 'I'm a loser; I should have studied', 'Tests without warning are so unfair.'

Ask one of the students to record answers for each scenario. You might like to alternate this role between members of the group. Follow the above steps for each of the scenarios listed on the cards.

B. Thought evaluations

Return to one of the scenarios discussed in Part A of this activity. For each of the thoughts ask students the following prompt questions:

❀ Could this fit into one of the categories of cognitive distortions (refer to the Common Thought Distortions on page 60)?

❀ How does this thought make you feel? Give this feeling a rating out of ten – one being equal to 'not very much' and ten being equal to 'extremely strong'. Use the Emotion Meter found on page 61 to support this.

❀ How would the feelings related to this thought make you behave?

❀ Is this a helpful or unhelpful thought?

❀ What if we chose another thought in relation to this scenario? Does the new thought make us feel any different? Does it make our emotional response any stronger or weaker?

Teaching tip

This aim of this activity is for students to grasp the concept that our feelings and behaviour do not occur in isolation and that they are products of our thoughts. The figure below might be useful to draw upon to demonstrate this point. You might also need to continue reinforcing that our thoughts influence what we feel and how we respond to any given situation.

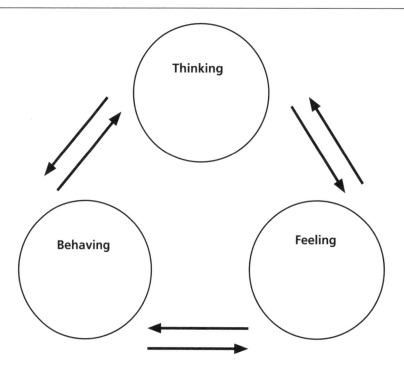

Activity 3: Refreshing reframes

Time: 15 minutes

Materials: Thought Cards (see page 62) and Emotion Meter (see page 61)

Instructions: Seat students in a circle with the Thought Cards spread face-down across the floor.

The key to this exercise is demonstrating how thoughts may be reframed. Begin this by introducing the concept of re-framing the thought. You can use the tipsheet titled Hot Tip Number 2: Positive Thinking found on page 63. The tipsheet will assist in revising the relationship between thoughts, feelings and behaviour and introduces the three-step process to challenging thinking.

Teaching tip

It is important to draw the students' attention to the three-step process to positive thinking. Students have already explored step 1 (awareness) and step 2 (evaluate) in the previous activity. The final component and purpose of this activity is teaching them how to reframe.

Three easy steps to positive thinking

1. STOP and listen to your self-talk. Have *awareness* of your self-talk.
2. Then *evaluate* your self-talk. Thinking of reasons why your thoughts might be false is a little harder, but will become a lot easier with practice. If it is too difficult to think of another perspective, it might help to ask someone who can be more objective about the task.
3. Lastly, *reframe* your self-talk so it is more truthful and positive.

Get students to take turns retrieving the Thought Cards. When a student has collected a card, ask him or her to read out the thought. As with Activity 2, ask the group to express how this thought might make them feel and how strongly they might experience this emotion (using the Emotion Meter).

Next, ask the group if it can come up with a way to replace or reframe the thought. The reframed thought needs to acknowledge the circumstances of the initial thought and be reframed in a way that is more helpful.

For example if an initial thought was:

'I failed maths; I am a loser' a reframed thought might be: 'While it is not ideal that I failed maths, I know that I did not study and I will try harder next time.'

Reflection

Ask the students to reflect on something they found really useful in this session related to their thinking. Provide students a few minutes to reflect on this question and then ask them to share their thoughts.

Individual instruction and homework activities

 Prior to beginning the following activities, provide each young person with the tipsheet Hot Tip Number 2: Positive Thinking (see page 63). Allow sufficient time for this to be read and discussed.

Activity 2.1: Thoughts and feelings

A. Consider the following situation:

Both you and your best friend, John, try out for a place in the local cricket team. You play cricket with John all the time and think you are both equally good players. You have played for the same number of years and feel like you both have the same skills. The coach chooses John to join his team and not you.

❀ Your first thoughts would be?
❀ You would feel?

What actually happened was this:

The coach only had one place in the team and had no specific reasons for choosing John over you. The coach rationalized that this would not matter, as there was a spot in the other team that you would be happy to take. Even though you wouldn't get to play with John, you have mates in the second team too.

❀ Given the new information, your first thoughts would be?
❀ You would feel?

B. Consider the following situation:

You were at the canteen at school and, as you passed a group from your class, they burst into laughter. They are the popular guys who wear the trendiest gear. You were wearing your old jeans and a white polo.

❀ Your first thoughts would be?
❀ You would feel?

What actually happened was:

One of the boys in the group had just finished telling the others a funny joke. They had been so intent on listening to the joke that many of the boys had not even seen you walk past.

❀ Given the new information, your first thoughts would be?
❀ You would feel?

Activity 2.2: Evaluate the evidence

A. Read the situation and evaluate the evidence.

You are on the train and a group of students in the year above you is sitting behind you. They start whispering and laughing.

Thought: 'They are talking about me – they must be making fun of my jumper. I knew I should not have worn it out of the house.'

Feelings: Anger, hurt, embarrassment.

Possible reasons self-talk may be true:

The jumper is quite old.

When you turned around they were looking at you.

You know one of the students in that group doesn't like you because you had a fight last year.

Possible reasons self-talk may be false:

They might be talking about something or someone else.

They just happen to be near you and facing in your direction.

That student probably hasn't held a grudge about a silly fight from a year ago.

B. How would thinking positively help you in this situation?

Activity 2.3: Change your thoughts

A. Recall the situation from before:

You are on the train and a group of students in the year above you is sitting behind you. They start whispering and laughing.

Old thought: 'They are talking about me – they must be making fun of my jumper.'

New thought: 'Some kids are whispering and laughing behind me. They might be…'
(complete the sentence in the space below).

_____

Old feelings: Anger, hurt, embarrassment.

New feelings:

_____

Activity 2.4: Challenge self-talk

A. Think of something that has happened to you which made you feel upset or disappointed in yourself. Have AWARENESS – listen to your self-talk (thoughts).

❀ What happened?
❀ What did you think?
❀ How did you feel?

B. EVALUATE your self-talk:

❀ Was it 100 per cent accurate?
❀ Were there other possibilities?
❀ What is the evidence *for* and *against*?
❀ Possible reasons self-talk may be true:
❀ Possible reasons self-talk may be false:

Recall your old thought(s) from above:

_____

New thought(s):

_____

Recall your old feeling(s) from above:

_____

New feeling(s):

_____

Modifying the activities for students with additional needs

Intrinsic self-reflection and monitoring of thoughts is difficult for some students. The following list of recommendations will assist in tailoring this module to students with additional needs:

1. Provide students with visual materials related to the way that thoughts influence feelings and behaviours. The figure on page 52 may be photocopied and laminated so that the student may carry around a portable version to act as a reminder at all times.

2. If the student is unable to understand the concept of self-reflection (i.e., an ability to challenge thoughts), then make the specific behaviour the focus. Use tools such as reward charts, token boards and self-monitoring (recording) sheets so that the specific behaviour that needs to be changed can be monitored and the changes reinforced if successful.

3. If the student is able to understand the concept of *thinking*, but lacks the ability to reframe, provide the reframed thought for them. This new thought could be one or two sentences written on the back of a business-size card so it can be kept and used when required.

Resources

These can be photocopied from the following pages
or downloaded from http://education.frydenberg.continuumbooks.com

Scenario cards

Photocopy cards onto good quality bond paper and cut out. These may be used again and are worth laminating.

You are in maths class and your teacher has just informed you that you will be doing a pop quiz. You have not been doing any homework.

You have to do an oral presentation to the whole year level.

A friend of yours is having a party at the weekend and has not invited you.

The teacher gave you a detention for arriving late to school three mornings in a row.

Your mum or dad (or care-giver) will not let you go to the shopping mall at the weekend with your best friend.

Common thought distortions

1. **All or nothing thinking**

   All or nothing thinking is when you see things as being either black or white. For example, 'Everybody hates me.'

2. **Over-generalization**

   This is characterized by phrases such as 'always' and 'never'. Over-generalization involves a tendency to view one or more negative events as part of a never-ending pattern of defeat. For example, 'I never play a good game of football.'

3. **Globalization**

   You pick out a single negative detail and this influences your whole view of the situation. For example: you performed in a play at school and received lots of praise for your efforts. However, one person criticized your performance. Globalization is where you focus on this one negative comment and conclude that your performance was 'dreadful.'

4. **Rejecting the positive**

   You discount positive experiences by insisting that they 'don't count'. For example, 'It was nothing – anyone can do that.'

5. **Jumping to conclusions**

   You interpret things negatively when there is no definite evidence to support your conclusion. This includes:

   Mind reading. Without assessing the evidence, you conclude that someone else is reacting negatively to you. For example, 'They think I'm a loser.'

   Fortune telling. You predict that things will turn out badly. For example: before a party you may tell yourself, 'I'm not going to know anybody there. I will have no one to talk to.'

6. **Catastrophizing**

   You predict that things will turn out badly regardless of past experience or evidence. You tend to think about the 'worst case scenario' for the event. For example, 'I am going to fail the test. It's going to be a disaster.'

7. **Magnification**

   You exaggerate the magnitude of your problems and shortcomings or you understate the importance of your desirable qualities. For example, 'I was lucky to have received an A in my maths test.' (attributing success to luck as opposed to your own ability).

8. **Emotional reasoning**

   You assume that your negative emotions necessarily reflect the way things really are. For example, 'I can't seem to do anything right, that is why I am feeling so down.'

9. **Shoulds (musts/oughts)**

   You tell yourself that things should be the way you wanted or expected them to be. This is characterized by the words 'should', 'must', 'ought to' and 'have to'. For example, 'All people should like me and treat me with the respect I deserve.'

10. **Personalization**

    Personalization occurs when you hold yourself personally responsible for an event that isn't entirely under your control. For example, 'Johnny left school and it is all my fault.'

Adapted (Burns, 1999; McMullin 2000; & Shiraldi, 2001)

10 – Boiling point

9 – Extremely strong

8 – Very strong

7 – Quite strong

6 – Strong

5 – Considerable

4 – To a degree

3 – Weak

2 – A little

1 – Not very much

Thought cards

Photocopy cards onto good quality bond paper and cut out. These may be used again and could be laminated.

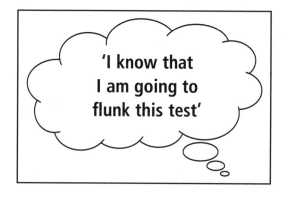

'I know that
I am going to
flunk this test'

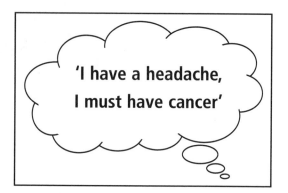

'I have a headache,
I must have cancer'

'If I do not get an A
in class, I will never
get into uni'

'Anybody that cannot
spell is stupid'

'Sarah should have
asked me to sit with
her at lunch time'

'I hate sport.
It is awful'

Tipsheet: Hot tip number 2: Positive thinking

Coping is your own unique and individual way of dealing with a problem or issue. There is no single formula for coping and the way we cope with a problem is dependent on the type of problem, the circumstances in which the problem or difficulty exists, and the unique needs of the individual. People can better deal with the vast range of difficulties and problems that may present themselves when they have an extended coping repertoire and can draw from a wide range of coping strategies. Positive thinking is an essential component in your coping repertoire. It is widely agreed that people who are able to think positively and challenge negative or irrational thoughts are typically happier and cope better with difficulties than those that don't. Our feelings are controlled by our thoughts and not by things that happen.

NEGATIVE THOUGHTS = NEGATIVE FEELINGS/HOPELESSNESS

POSITIVE THOUGHTS = POSITIVE FEELINGS/HOPE

Each day hundreds of thoughts run through our minds, explaining and judging events and situations. If the thoughts are mostly negative, then we will be experiencing mostly negative feelings

Negative thinking can cause
- ❀ Low self-esteem
- ❀ Frustration and anger with self and others
- ❀ A negative view of everything in life
- ❀ Unhappiness/depression
- ❀ Hopelessness
- ❀ Poor health
- ❀ Poor performance in sports, at school, etc.
- ❀ Low motivation

How to think more positively
When something happens that you have negative feelings about, *evaluate your thoughts*. Look at why the thought may not be true and try to reframe it to make it more truthful. This involves changing it so that it is less negative. You don't have to pretend not to be disappointed or hurt about situations – that would be unnatural.

The aim here is to try to look at the most positive perspective and keep some hope in your thoughts. One negative event doesn't make your whole future negative.

Three easy steps to positive thinking
1. STOP and listen to your self-talk. Have awareness of your self-talk. A good way to do this is to write down:
    - ❀ The thing or event that happened
    - ❀ What your thoughts were
    - ❀ How you felt
2. Then evaluate your self-talk. Make a LIST of 'why your self-talk might be true' and 'why your self-talk might be false'. Thinking of reasons why your thoughts might be false is a little harder, but will become a lot easier with practice. If it is too difficult to think of another perspective, it might help to ask someone else who can be more objective.
3. Lastly, REFRAME your self-talk so it is more truthful and positive.

Coping quiz

1. What are the three steps to positive thinking?
2. Why is it important to challenge our thoughts if they are negative or unhelpful?
3. Jane is a Year 9 student who has a best friend called Jess. On the weekend she knows that Jess is going to the movies with another friend called Sam. Jane is thinking 'Jess hates me, she doesn't want to be my friend anymore'.

   a) How would these thoughts make Jane feel?

   b) How would these thoughts make Jane behave?

   c) How would you evaluate these thoughts? What evidence is there?

   d) How could you reframe these thoughts?

Further reading

Burns, D. E. (1999), *The Feeling Good Handbook*. New York: Plume.

Shiraldi, G. R. (2001), *The Self-Esteem Workbook*. West: New Harbinger Publications.

Stallard, P. (2002), *Think Good – Feel Good. A Cognitive Behaviour Therapy Workbook for Children and Young People*. Chichester: John Wiley and Sons.

Module 3 – Strategies that don't help

'I cope with work by trying not to fall behind'

Molly, 16

Learning outcomes

The aim of this module is to raise awareness of the ineffective coping strategies that people use and to explore some productive alternatives. By the end of this module students will be able to identify the different types of non-productive coping strategies they engage in and how these may negatively affect their thoughts and behaviour.

In this session students will:

❧ Explore the different types of non-productive coping and how these may manifest
❧ Be able to describe which non-productive strategies are presently being used and how they can be reduced or replaced

Instructor's notes

No coping strategy is inherently good or bad. It is the context in which they are used or the extent to which they are used that makes strategies non-productive. For example, a little worrying might spur one into action, while too much worrying can leave one immobilized and resisting action. Use of non-productive coping strategies in adolescent populations can stem from many causes: poor adult modelling, mental health issues, a deficit in coping education, poor resources, low self-esteem, and low self-efficacy, that is, a lack of belief in one's own capacities. Non-productive coping may lead to negative psychological sequelae such as emotional distress (e.g., anxiety and depression) and place a young person at significant risk. Regardless of the ineffective, dangerous or reckless nature of non-productive coping strategies they are still used by many young people to help cope with setbacks they encounter.

Common non-productive coping observed during adolescence includes:

Worrying
Self-blame
Tension reduction (smoking, drugs and alcohol)
Ignoring the problem
Keeping the problem to oneself
Declaring that one can't cope
Getting sick
Giving up

While non-productive coping strategies are coping strategies in their own right, it is important for young people to realize that these methods are often a source of anxiety, depression, stress, distress, exaggeration of the problem and an inability to concentrate. With the aid of psychoeducational opportunities and a willingness to change, non-productive coping strategies can be mitigated or even replaced by a more productive repertoire.

Setting the context

This module aims to explore non-productive coping and its negative impact on wellbeing and happiness. Some of the non-productive coping strategies that will be explored are in common use by many adolescents. Others, however, are used less often. To set the context of this module, begin by reflecting on the Module 2 (Positive thinking) and reiterate the connection between thinking, feeling and behaviour. The cognitive behavioural emphasis of this module sets a solid foundation for discussing non-productive strategies and their possible genesis. It might be useful to re-draw the following figure demonstrating the relationship between thoughts, feelings and behaviours, both to remind students and to refer to during discussions.

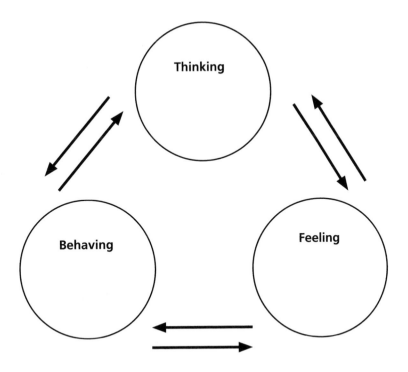

Group and classwork activities

Ice breaker: Positive feelings

Time: 10 minutes

Materials: None

Instructions: Sit students in a circle with one member of the group sitting in the centre of the circle with eyes closed. Explain to the students that one approach to feeling good about ourselves is by making somebody else feel special. We might do this by expressing gratitude for a generous act, letting someone know our positive feelings towards them, or by offering a small gesture such as a helping hand when someone least expects it. In this activity students will take turns around the circle to say one positive thing about the student in the middle. Ask students to focus on the personality or talents of the individual, as opposed to physical appearance or the recipient's possessions. This activity is completed when each student has had a turn in the middle. Ensure you allow enough time for every student to have a turn.

Activity 1: Sorting against strife

Time: 25 minutes

Materials: Coping Cards from Module 1 (see page 39)

Instructions: To revise previous modules, ask students to recall the three categories into which coping styles fit: productive, non-productive and reference to others. Once this has been established, ask the students to sort the Coping Cards into these three categories. Allow discussion to take place as the students organize the cards into three piles. By the end of the exercise the piles should reflect the following groupings:

PRODUCTIVE	NON-PRODUCTIVE	REFERENCE TO OTHERS
☐ Focus on solving the problem	☐ Not coping	☐ Invest in close friends
☐ Work hard and achieve	☐ Worry	☐ Seek social support
☐ Focus on the positive	☐ Ignore the problem	☐ Seek professional help
☐ Seek relaxing diversions	☐ Wishful thinking	☐ Try to be funny
☐ Physical recreation	☐ Tension reduction	☐ Seek spiritual support
☐ Accept my best efforts	☐ Self-blame	☐ Seek to belong
	☐ Get sick	☐ Social action
	☐ Give up	
	☐ Keep to self	
	☐ Act up	

The next step of this activity is to remove the non-productive Coping Cards only. If you are working with a large group, divide students into smaller groups, as the next step of this activity works best with smaller groups of students. Ask the students to sort the ten non-productive coping strategies in order from the highest risk to the lowest risk. When talking about *risk* we are determining those factors that are the most detrimental to an individual's general wellbeing. Provide students with a solid amount of time to sort their cards, encouraging discussion and rationalization for choices made. Remind students that there are no right or wrong answers. Once the non-productive Coping Cards have been sorted, ask the students to share their responses. You might like to use the following prompt questions:

❀ Of the non-productive coping styles, which did you rate as being the most risky? Why?
❀ Which did you rate as causing the least amount or risk? Why?
❀ Of the ten, which do you think adolescents use the most?
❀ Why do you think adolescents use non-productive coping?

Activity 2: Causes to cope

Time: 10 minutes

Materials: Causes to Cope worksheet (see page 73)

Instructions: Provide students with the Causes to Cope worksheet. Ask students to complete the sheet, identifying recent triggers or setbacks they may have experienced that might have caused them to use a coping strategy (whether productive or non-productive). In order for students to feel comfortable, only call on those who are happy and willing to share their responses.

To close this session, explain to students that there are many reasons young people engage in non-productive coping. The main reasons being:

- It is a habit
- The person might not be aware when the strategy is not useful, perhaps even harmful
- The person may not be aware of the range of strategies that they could use, so they just go with what they know

Give students a minute to recall which non-productive coping strategies they have used in the past and to reflect upon the possible reasons for the strategy they adopted.

Activity 3: Reasons to change

Time: 10 minutes

Materials: Reasons to Change worksheet (see page 74)

Instructions: Provide students with a copy of the worksheet. Allow 10 minutes for students to complete this activity. This is another self-reflection exercise as in Activity 2; students should only share their responses should they feel comfortable.

Teaching tip

Students learn best when they come to their own conclusions about why they engage in a particular behaviour. Encourage them to see the negative consequences associated with non-productive coping. Establish whether there is enough reason to change. For those students who engage in little non-productive coping, reinforce the point that *everybody* can improve the way they deal with setbacks; there is always room for improvement!

Reflection

Ask students to spend some time reflecting on this session and what they can change in their lives to make them more productive *copers*. Ask them to share their responses.

Individual instruction and homework activities

 Prior to beginning the following activities, provide each young person with the tipsheet titled Hot Tip Number 3: Strategies that Don't Help on page 75. The tipsheet provides a summary of the non-productive coping strategies explored in this module. Allow sufficient time for this to be read and discussed.

Activity 3.1: Unhelpful ways to cope

Self-talk is how we explain and understand things to ourselves. It is another way to describe the thoughts that we have. What we say to ourselves to explain events or understand things that have happened. Self-talk can affect our feelings and behaviour. Negative self-talk may make us feel hopeless, while positive self-talk may make us feel hopeful.

A. Here is Emet's situation.

Situation: Emet would like to go for a leadership position at school and will have to do a speech at assembly. He is thinking, 'I can't do a speech; it will be terrible. I give up.'

Emet giving up is an example of non-productive coping. Can you think of other examples? Write them down.

How would you reframe this positively?

B. List some of the results of worrying.

C. What are some other positive ways that you use, or that other people may use, to stop worrying or to reduce stress? Write them down.

D. Write down other negative strategies that you can think of that young people might use to try and relieve stress.

What are some of the effects of using these negative tension reduction strategies
On the problem? The individual? Others?

E. Describe some things that have happened that you have blamed yourself for.

Now consider these situations:

Situation: Jason's school lost the debating team competition. Jason thinks: 'We lost the competition because I didn't know what to say.'

Why is it unhelpful for Jason to self-blame?

What sort of feelings will self-blame cause for Jason?

Situation: Harry was collecting the assignments for his class and he tripped. Papers went everywhere. Harry thinks: 'Its all my fault, I'm so clumsy! Everyone will think I'm an idiot.'

Why is it unhelpful for Harry to use self-blame?

What sort of feelings will self-blame cause for Harry?

Situation: Sarah borrowed her mum's necklace. Her younger sister took it from her room and lost it at school. Sarah blames herself for the necklace being lost.

Why is it unhelpful – even harmful – for Sarah to use self-blame?

What sort of feelings will self-blame cause for Sarah?

What positive approach could you take if you did have some responsibility in a problem?

What might be the resulting feelings?

Think of a friendship that went wrong. What happened?

How could it have turned out differently?

F. Consider the following situations:

Situation: Sean has been spending a lot of time at the local skateboard ramp skating with friends after school. Sean has an assignment due in one week. He was given the outline six weeks ago and has not made a start. He thinks it is too late to do anything about it now.

List some of the possible results of ignoring this problem.

Situation: Hannah called out to Tracy in the school playground, but Tracy did not hear her and kept walking. Hannah thinks that Tracy ignored her and spent the rest of the day in the library because she feels that without Tracy she has no-one to hang out with.

What do you think would have happened if Hannah went out into the school playground during lunch break and found Tracy?

Was ignoring the problem a good coping strategy?

What might have been a better strategy?

Situation: Simon sits next to Josh in class. Simon finds Josh frustrating as he always interrupts him with continuous chatter. The teachers often tell Simon off for talking, even though it is always Josh who is talking to Simon. Simon tries to ignore Josh and does not say anything to the teacher in case he gets Josh into trouble.

What might happen if Simon continues to ignore Josh in this situation?

How could Simon have dealt with things differently?

What or who could have helped Simon to deal with this situation differently?

G. Can you think of a situation when ignoring the problem might be the best way to deal with it? Write it down.

Activity 3.2: Non-productive coping strategies

The non-productive coping strategies are:

Not cope

Worry

Self-blame

Ignore the problem

Keep problems to self

Wishful thinking

Tension reduction (negative strategies to reduce stress and tension, e.g., smoking)

Get sick

Give up

A. Think of a situation at school in which a person (real or imagined) used a non-productive coping strategy.

What happened?

Suggest a more positive coping strategy that might have worked well in the situation.

B. Now think of a situation at home in which a person (real or imagined) used a non-productive coping strategy.

What happened?

Suggest a more positive coping strategy that might have worked well in the situation.

C. Now, think of a situation outside of school and home in which a person (real or imagined) used a non-productive coping strategy.

What happened?

Suggest a more positive coping strategy that might have worked well in the situation.

Modifying the activities for students with additional needs

Taking the tipsheet titled Hot Tip Number 3: Strategies that Don't Help (see page 75) as a framework, use role-play to demonstrate the different non-productive coping strategies used by young people. It may be helpful to modify your language for this topic. Rather than say 'non-productive', it may be easier to explain the terminology as being 'helpful' and 'unhelpful'.

As this module specifically looks at non-productive coping strategies, one of the main aims is to teach students the coping language used to describe strategies that are not helpful. Continuing on from Module 1, you may find it useful to further develop the students' coping language through:

❀ Creating coping word searches (e.g., find-a-words)
❀ Creating jumbled coping word activities (e.g., anagrams)
❀ Name to picture matching activities (e.g., card games)
❀ Playing hangman with coping words
❀ Creating posters of cool friend behaviour vs uncool friend behaviour or good listening vs bad listening

Resources

These can be photocopied from the following pages
or downloaded from http://education.frydenberg.continuumbooks.com

Causes to cope

Spend some time reflecting on the setbacks and issues you have encountered over the last year. Write these down and consider whether or not you used a productive, non-productive or reference to other strategy. Was this effective? Would you do the same?

Setback (Describe time(s) when you felt that you were challenged or faced with a significant issue)	Coping strategy used	Was this effective?	Would you use it again? If no, what would you do instead?

Reasons to change

---

1. Non-productive strategies I have used:	2. Advantages of non-productive strategies:

4. Reasons to change non-productive coping in favour of more productive coping:	3. Disadvantages of non-productive strategies:

Tipsheet: Hot tip number 3: Strategies that don't help

The way we cope can be generally divided into two different types of strategies:

1. Productive (helpful) coping
2. Non-productive (not helpful) coping.

Some commonly used coping strategies are generally not helpful in dealing with problems.

A person may rely on these useless strategies because:

❀ They are a HABIT
❀ The person might not be aware when the strategy is useless, perhaps even harmful
❀ The person may not be aware of the range of strategies that they could use, so they just go with what they know

Unhelpful coping includes:

Not cope
Worry
Self-blame
Ignore the problem
Keep problem to self
Tension reduction (strategies to reduce stress and tension, e.g., smoking, being naughty)
Wishful thinking
Get sick
Give up

You can avoid non-productive coping!

You can begin to reduce your use of non-productive strategies by:

❀ Recognizing that some strategies that you might be using are not helpful
❀ Thinking of more helpful strategies that might be helpful in the situation
❀ Decreasing stress

Quick tips to avoid non-productive coping

1. **Avoid self-blame**. Instead, learn from your mistakes and work out how to do things differently next time.
2. **Engage in peaceful activities**: relaxation, fishing, walking, reading, taking a bath, etc.
3. **Try to do more activities you enjoy**: drawing, board games, computer games, playing music, watching a movie or favourite television show, etc.
4. **Make sure you make time for physical exercise**. Go for a run, go to the gym, go skipping, punch a punching bag, dance to your favourite music…whatever you find most relaxing and enjoyable.

Coping quiz

1. Why do young people use non-productive coping?
2. What is self-blame and why is this a non-productive strategy?
3. When would be an appropriate time to use self-blame? Think of an example or scenario.

Further reading

Gilbert, P. (1997), *Overcoming Depression*. London: Robinson.

MoodGYM, *A free self help program to teach cognitive behaviour therapy skills to people vulnerable to depression and anxiety. www.moodgym.anu.edu.au/*

Rowe, D. (1983), *Depression: The Way Out of Your Own Prison*. London: Routledge.

Tanner, S., & Basil, J. (1989), *Beating the Blues: A Self-help Approach to Overcoming* Depression. London: Sheldon Press.

Vernon, A. (2002), *What Works When With Children and Adolescents: A Handbook of Individual Counselling Techniques*. Champaign: Research Press.

Module 4 – Getting along with others

'I think friends and family are very important to me, I'm not usually that fussed over having the latest clothes, it all comes down to who you are. I just like being able to do sport and have some free time.'

Jason, 16

Contents

Learning outcomes

The aim of this module is to explore and practise skills related to communication and listening. This module will introduce students to mechanisms of effective communication and how they can become effective communicators through assertive communication and non-verbal communication skills.

In this session students will:

❀ Explore and practise concepts related to assertive communication
❀ Role-play listening skills

❀ Gain an increased understanding of the role of body language in communication and how other non-verbal cues can influence what we are saying

Instructor's notes

Effective communication is an essential part of coping with everyday life. There are many skills associated with effective communication and these will be explored over the next two modules. This module will explore basic communication skills: assertive communication, active listening and non-verbal communication. Module 5 will look at applying these skills, initiating and approaching communication, as well as seeking the appropriate avenues of professional help when needed.

Setting the context

A module that is titled Getting Along with Others and is based on teaching communication skills offers the opportunity for instructors to reflect upon their own performance as effective communicators. The individual instructor is just as important as appropriate lighting, temperature, privacy and space when setting the context for a session. Presentation, demeanour, and organization are all critical to an effective session. Communication skills are also a key element and provide an opportunity to model appropriate verbal and non-verbal communication skills to the student group.

Some points to consider when communicating with young people in a group setting:

❀ Are you speaking clearly enough? (e.g., using age appropriate language, speaking loud enough)
❀ Are your non-verbal cues appropriate? (e.g., facing the class)
❀ Are you allowing students to speak? Is there conversation taking place?
❀ Do you have a good rapport with students?
❀ Are you listening when students speak?
❀ Is the rate at which the session is delivered too fast or too slow?
❀ Do students understand the content of the session? Are modifications necessary?
❀ Are you allowing yourself planning time as well as personal reflection time after the session?

Group and classwork activities

Ice breaker: Coping is a juggling act
Time: 10 minutes

Materials: Six balloons. Depending on the size of your group, you may decide to use more.

Instructions: On each of the balloons write a word that may be regarded as a stressor. Some ideas include:

❀ Loss
❀ Homework

❀ Conflict with parents
❀ Work

❀ Exams

❀ Stress

❀ Fight with friends

❀ School

❀ Socializing

The methodology of this game is simple. Provide students with a large space and one of the balloons. Students are to keep the balloon in the air and not let it touch the ground. Run a trial of this activity for 3 minutes and stop the group to reflect on how well the activity went. Some prompt questions might include:

❀ Is more than one person trying to save the balloon at one time? Is this problematic?

❀ What can we do to avoid running into to each other? (e.g., call out other people's names, stay calm, speak loudly and clearly but don't yell, etc.)

Run the activity a second time but, this time, add more balloons. Again, students are required to prevent the balloons from touching the ground. You can add as many balloons as you like to make the activity increasingly more difficult. The harder this activity becomes, the more students will need to communicate effectively and work as a team in order to complete the activity successfully. Praise students for effective communication.

Follow this activity with a discussion about how the balloons in the activity represented stressful events in a person's life and how these can be managed through help from other people and good communication skills.

Teaching tip

Effective communication is a coping strategy that helps us get along better with our peers and other important people around us every day. In the previous activity we learnt that sometimes setbacks or stressors can build up. However, we are able to juggle them and deal with them more effectively when we:

1. Use effective communication

2. Seek appropriate help from those around us.

Activity 1: Non-verbal communication first aid

Time: 25 minutes

Materials: Non-verbal Communication Cards (see page 85), handout entitled Non-verbal Cues that Help Us Communicate (see page 87)

Instructions: Read through the handout as a group and discuss the ways in which people communicate without using words.

Following the group discussion, instruct the students to sit in a circle. To run the activity, students take turns to choose a Non-verbal Communication Card and, from the middle of the circle, act out the phrase on the card. The phrases are all related to feelings of being overwhelmed and not coping. First aid is provided to the student when the student group correctly guesses which phrase the student is acting out.

Activity 2: Are they listening?
Time: 20 minutes

Materials: None

Instructions: Ask the students to spend some time on the following two questions:

1. Are you approachable?
2. If one of your friends or family members had a problem, could they talk to you?

You might like to use the following script to explain the importance of listening skills:

> We would all like to think we are good listeners, but sometimes our words and behaviours can make it difficult for others to confide in us. People may not talk to others about their problems if they think that others might:

❀ Judge them
❀ Criticize them
❀ Not understand
❀ Dump them as a friend
❀ Break their confidence (i.e., gossip about their problem to others)
❀ Blame them

> Being a good listener means listening with an open ear and trying to understand an issue from another's point of view. This will make it easier for other people to talk to you about things that are important to them.

Ask to brainstorm the key features of a good listener. Ensure your list reflects the following:

❀ Good eye contact
❀ Appropriate body posture (facing the speaker, leaning towards the speaker)
❀ Thinking about what the speaker is saying
❀ Encouraging further talk through:
   — Reflecting on what the speaker is saying and adding anecdotes and comments (e.g., 'Uh huh', 'Yes', 'Really?')
   — Asking questions related to the topic

Next, ask the students to form pairs and role-play the following scenarios in turn. For each scenario, one member of the pair can be the talker, the other the listener. Encourage students to swap roles within each scenario. Make sure you, as the instructor, walk around the room to provide feedback. Ensure that students involved in the listening role are practising all the features of a good listener previously discussed.

1. You have just been told that your favourite aunt is moving to live in another country. You are really close to her and do not want her to leave.
2. You have not seen your dog for three days and you are really worried about his safety.
3. You have just received news that you have won a huge amount of money.

Complete this exercise by discussing the following questions:

1. When you were in the talking role, did you feel listened to?
2. What was it about your listener that helped you feel comfortable (or not comfortable) talking?

Teaching tip

Listening skills are vital for effective communication. In order for students to communicate effectively, they need to establish efficient listening skills. The function of this activity is to demonstrate that communication is a *two-way* street and listening skills are just as important as verbal and non-verbal communication.

Explain to the students that listening is a social skill and is vital in forming and maintaining relationships with peers.

Activity 3: Assertive communication

Time: 20 minutes

Materials: The tipsheet titled Hot Tip Number 4: Getting Along with Others (see page 89) and Scenario Cards (see page 88)

Instructions: Provide students with the tipsheet and read through this handout as a group.

With students seated in a circle, ask two volunteer students to stand in the middle of the circle and take a Scenario Card. The volunteer students act out the scenario using assertive, aggressive or non-assertive communication.

According to Powell (2000), assertive communicators express themselves and stand up for their values, rights and beliefs. They assert themselves in a firm, but polite manner. Aggressive communicators use aggressive means to communicate ideas; they might intimidate or belittle the person they are communicating with. They tend to be over-expressive and may raise their voice. Non-assertive communicators are permissive, inhibited and avoid speaking up when they need to. The may use a mildly raised voice, withdraw or attend to avoid expressing the point of view. Further details on assertive communication can be obtained from the tipsheet on page 89.

The student will act out a communication style depending on the instructions stated on the card. Students in the group should guess the style adopted and advise how the message could be re-communicated using assertive communication. The volunteer students may then act out the scenario again using an assertive style, based on the feedback given by the other students. Even if the original scenario called for assertive communication, there may have been improvements suggested by others in the group that could be used by a second role-play. Continue selecting volunteer students until all Scenario Cards have been used.

Reflection

Allow some time for the students to reflect upon the various facets of communication skills that were covered in the session. Ask them to consider one skill they would like to improve and invite them to share it with the rest of the group.

Individual instruction and homework activities

 If not already done, prior to beginning the following activities, provide each your person with tipsheet titled Hot Tip Number 4: Getting Along with Others on page 88. Allow sufficient time for this to be read and discussed.

Activity 4.1: Being assertive

A. Think of some aggressive, non-assertive and assertive responses for the following situations.

Situation: Your friends have bought alcohol to school. You don't like the taste of it and know that you could get into serious trouble if you get caught with it. Your friends tell you to have a drink and you don't want to. They tease you.

    Aggressive response:

    Non-assertive response:

    Assertive response:

Situation: A student walks past you in the corridor and accidentally knocks you, causing you to drop all your pens and papers on the ground.

    Aggressive response:

    Non-assertive response:

    Assertive response:

Activity 4.2: Body language

A. What's the definition of non-verbal communication?

B. Look at the body language in each of these cartoons. Is the body language suggesting that they are someone you could talk to? Why or why not?

Modifying the activities for students with additional needs

The best way to teach to students with additional needs the concept of effective communication and getting along with others is within a social setting. Consider running a social skills group, using board games, card games and activities that provide an opportunity to teach social skills with other students. You may find that you will need to modify the activities greatly to suit the specific needs of the students. To do this, consider using some of the social skills books listed in Further Reading on page 90.

Resources

These can be photocopied from the following pages
or downloaded from http://education.frydenberg.continuumbooks.com

Non-verbal communication cards

Photocopy these cards and cut them out. As these cards can be used again, laminating them might be useful.

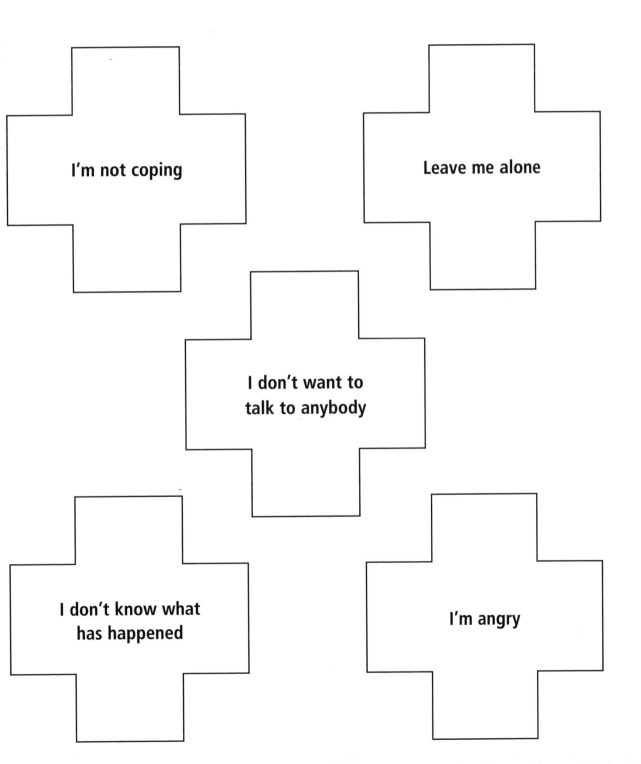

I'm not coping

Leave me alone

I don't want to talk to anybody

I don't know what has happened

I'm angry

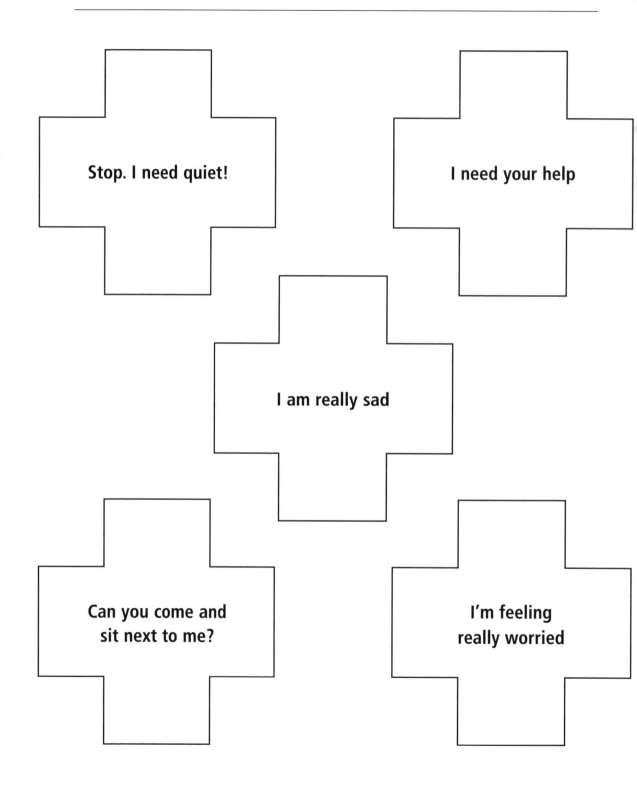

Stop. I need quiet!

I need your help

I am really sad

Can you come and
sit next to me?

I'm feeling
really worried

Non-verbal cues that help us communicate

Eye contact
- Look directly at the person as you speak. This will show you are sincere.
- Looking down or away may suggest that you are uncomfortable, that you lack confidence or that you are lying.
- Don't stare: this makes others uncomfortable.

Body posture
- Be comfortable and turn your upper body toward the person you are speaking to.
- Leaning, slumping or rocking sends a message of non-assertiveness.

Voice
- Keep it controlled and clear.
- Speak at a normal pace and volume.
- Avoid hesitating or saying 'umm' or you will appear uncertain.
- Don't use big words to try to impress people – especially if you use them incorrectly!

Facial expressions
- Sometimes people laugh to hide the fact that they are nervous. If you do this, people will not take you seriously. They may even be annoyed.
- Your expression must match the seriousness of your message.

Physical distance
- The distance will depend on your relationship with the person. If you are too close or you make physical contact you may invade the other person's personal space or send them the message that you wish to become more intimate.

Scenario cards

Photocopy and cut out the following scenario cards. You may choose to laminate these cards for future use.

You have gone to your friend's house and their parents have made you tuna sandwiches for lunch. You hate tuna!

Person 1: Plays friend's mother
Person 2: Plays tuna-hater

Use aggressive communication

The lady at the canteen shortchanged you.

Person 1: Plays canteen lady
Person 2: Plays shortchanged student

Use non-assertive communication

You are at a café and the waitress brings you a plate of food that you did not order.

Person 1: Plays waitress
Person 2: Plays person who got the wrong food

Use aggressive communication

Your best friend forgets to return the CD you lent her.

Person 1: Plays best friend
Person 2: Plays CD lender

Use non-assertive communication

Your teacher asks you to act out a scenario and you don't want to.

Person 1: Plays teacher
Person 2: Plays student who does not want to act

Use aggressive communication

Your teacher gives you an F for your maths test and you don't understand what went wrong.

Person 1: Plays teacher
Person 2: Plays student with an F

Use assertive communication

Your parents won't let you go to the shopping mall at the weekend.

Person 1: Plays mum or dad
Person 2: Plays shop-a-holic

Use aggressive communication

Tipsheet: Hot tip number 4: Getting along with others

Communication is a part of everyday life. We use it to join a group, make a friend or to reveal our deepest thoughts, feelings or fears. Sometimes it can be difficult to communicate with someone, particularly if you want to talk about an issue that has been on your mind. If you feel that you can't speak with someone about a problem, try talking about an issue that is less concerning and see how it goes.

In time you may feel comfortable to discuss your problem, or you may decide to talk with someone else about it. If you continue to experience difficulties with talking to other people, it may be useful to tell someone about the fact that you find it hard to reach out – school counsellors, psychologists and help lines will be understanding and can help you with some ways to get started.

When you want to talk to someone about something that is important to you, how you approach the conversation may have an impact on how well the conversation goes. To make it easier to approach or reach out to others, you first need to have it clear in your mind what you want to express (feelings and words) to the other person. Then, you need to say it in a way without putting the other person down. One way of communicating successfully is by using assertive communication.

People can communicate in three ways:

1. Aggressive
2. Non-assertive
3. Assertive

Aggressive

This is where a person stands up for their rights in a rude and overly powerful manner. It is an attack on another person, rather than objecting to their behaviour or the situation. It is often an over-reaction to the situation and includes degrading others or making them responsible for your anger. (It's OK to feel angry and to let others know how you feel, but this can be done assertively).

Non-assertive

This behaviour includes feeling sorry for yourself, not standing up for your rights and remaining silent so that others do not know how you feel. It can also include trying to get others to do what you want in a roundabout way.

For example:

- ❀ Using guilt, such as saying, 'After all I've done for you...'
- ❀ Being non-co-operative or unsupportive of the other person, hoping that they will guess how you feel or to wear down their enthusiasm
- ❀ Ruining other people's pleasure by complaining or criticizing, hoping that others will guess how you feel
- ❀ Avoiding decisions and responsibility by being non-assertive, such as saying, 'You decide/whatever you want.'

Assertive

Assertive communication is:

❀ Where you stand up for your rights

❀ Expressing how you feel in a way that does not put others down

❀ Honest

❀ Respectful

To communicate assertively, use 'I messages' or assertive statements, such as:

❀ Start with 'I' followed by a statement of your feeling (e. g., 'I feel upset...')

❀ State a tangible situation (e.g. '...that I am not allowed to go out with my friends.')

❀ Include an explanation of effect, or why the situation gives rise to the feelings (e.g., 'It makes me feel left out.')

WARNING: Watch your non-verbal communication!

Non-verbal communication is essentially the way we communicate without words. We do this through:

❀ Gestures (such as pointing)

❀ Facial expressions (such as smiling, frowning)

❀ Body and eye movements (such as hugging, shrugging shoulders, looking away)

These all convey signals that others use to interpret our messages, thoughts and feelings.

Coping quiz

1. How can you tell if someone is listening to you?

2. Why is knowing about non-verbal communication important?

3. True or false: assertive communication is that which expresses your needs and how you feel without putting somebody else down.

Further reading

Alberti, R. & Emmons, M. (1974), *Your Perfect Right.* Sans Luis Obispo: Impact.

Cohen-Posey, K. (1995), *How to Handle Bullies, Teasers, and Other Meanies.* New York: Rainbow Books.

Fennel, M. (1999), *Overcoming Low Self Esteem.* London: Robinson.

Fuller, A. (2003), *From Surviving to Thriving: Promoting Mental Health in Young People.* Melbourne: The Australian Council for Educational Research.

Graham, R. S., Rees, S. (1991), Assertiveness Training. London: Routledge.

Powell, T. (2000), *The Mental Health Handbook.* Oxford: Speechmark Publishing.

Shiraldi, G. R. (2001), *The Self-Esteem Workbook.* West: New Harbinger Publications.

For students with additional needs

Baker, J. (2006), *Social Skills Picture Book for High School and Beyond.* Arlington: Future Horizons.

Firth, N., Frydenberg, E. & Greaves, D. (2006), 'Shared needs: Teachers helping students with learning disabilities to cope more effectively'. *Understanding Teacher Stress in an Age of Accountability.* Volume 111 in 'Research on Stress and Coping in Education'. Greenwich: Information Age Publishing.

Mense, B., Debney, S., & Druce, T (2005), *Ready, Set, Remember: Short-term Auditory Memory Activities.* Camberwell: ACER Press.

Module 5 – Asking for help

'He who is afraid of asking is ashamed of learning.'

Danish proverb

Contents

Group and classwork activities
Individual instruction and homework activities
Modifying the activities for students with additional needs 96
Resources
Coping quiz 99
Further reading 99

Learning outcomes

The aim of this module is to raise awareness of the importance of reaching out, both to others and to available networks and supports. By the end of this module students will have a greater understanding of the mechanisms behind asking for help.

In this session students will:

❀ Be exposed to some of the difficulties young people face when asking for help
❀ Practise asking for help and explore a wide range of issues for which young people may require assistance, whether it be from friends, families or professionals
❀ Be introduced to the various roles and functions of the professionals available to help young people
❀ Be provided with a list of telephone and online resources

Instructor's notes

The ability to seek help is critical for wellbeing, psycho-social adjustment and productive coping in young people. An important aim of this module is to provide young people with the skills they need to actively engage in help-seeking behaviour. Once equipped with the confidence and resources to engage in help-seeking, young people often experience an improvement in their mental health (Rickwood, Deane, Wilson, & Ciarrochi, 2005). This module follows on from the themes of effective communication raised in the previous module. Students need basic communication skills to approach another person for help. This module aims to provide students with information about the people and professionals available to assist them. It also equips students with the basic interpersonal skills they need when deciding upon the appropriate means by which to access help (i.e., face to face, telephone or internet).

Setting the context

It is important first to remind students about the limits of confidentiality that apply to certain individuals. Teachers, family, friends or trusted significant adults are not necessarily bound by confidentiality. However, they are useful people to ask for help when needed. Professionals such as psychologists are bound by confidentiality except when the issues at hand raise significant legal or safety concerns.

It is important too that students be aware of their own responsibilities with regard to confidentiality. The health and safety of others must always take precedence over confidentiality. If, for example, a friend shares information that indicates they are at risk, students must understand the importance of seeking outside help, irrespective of confidentiality.

Group and classwork activities

Ice breaker: Balloon pass

Time: 10 minutes

Materials: Balloons (one per two students)

Instructions: Students form pairs and each pair is given a balloon. Ask students to line up at one end of the room. Instruct them to carry the balloon with their partner to the other side of the room as fast as they can without dropping it. The only catch is they must carry the balloon using only their stomachs; no hands allowed! You might like to adapt this activity so that student pairs must carry the balloon with shoulders, knees, cheeks, bottoms or elbows.

This activity requires calm and considered effective communication. It also requires the members of each pair to use skills related to helping.

Activity 1: Jumbled instructions

Time: 40 minutes

Materials: Small, miscellaneous objects such as scissors, glue, sticky tape, pencils (one object per student pair). Pens and paper

Instructions: Instruct students to form pairs, making sure each student is partnering a student they do not usually work with. Name one member of the pair Partner A and the other Partner B. The role of Partner A is to find a miscellaneous object somewhere in the room and hide it without Partner B seeing it (you might like to send the Partner Bs out of the room).

Partner A then writes down a list of instructions as to how Partner B may find the object (e.g., stand up, walk to the door, lift up the table lid, look under the lid, etc.). Ensure that Partner A writes the directions in a list format as the next step requires them to cut out each sentence and jumble up the instructions. When the Student Bs return, their role is to decipher the directions by placing them in order and then find the hidden object.

Ask the students to swap roles and repeat the exercise.

Teaching tip

The aim of this activity is to teach students the importance of organization. Follow this activity by a group discussion with students seated in a circle. Use the following prompt questions to create discussion:

1. What did you find hard about this activity?
2. What did you find easy?
3. Have you ever approached someone with an issue and not quite known what to say or how to say it?

Emphasize the importance of organizing thoughts. Inform students that to make yourself clearly understood it is often useful to plan what you are going to say and to organize the sequence of your thoughts. When the sentences were jumbled the content was still there, yet the instructions were difficult to understand. Organization is essential to ensure your listener understands your intended message clearly.

Activity 2: Helpful helpers

Time: 40 minutes

Materials: Tipsheet Hot Tip Number 5: Asking for Help (see page 97)

Instructions: Have students form groups of three and read through the tipsheet. Allow them sufficient time to read the tipsheet and discuss the content with each other.

Next, ask the student groups to devise a scenario in which a young person may seek help. They may need a few minutes for discussion.

The next step is to ask the students to consider whom they would ask for help and how they would ask for help. In addition, ask them to consider if any other people would be involved. Would they have a support person, for example? Once the scenario and details have been planned, provide students with some time to act out their scenario to the rest of the group.

Discussion

At the end of the exercise, students will have been exposed to a variety of scenarios in which a young person might require help as well as the avenues by which they might seek it. Provide students with some discussion time after the exercise. You might like to use the following questions:

1. What was one thing you learnt from observing the groups during this session?
2. Do you think help-seeking is hard or easy?
3. What are some issues that young people face today?
4. When can help-seeking be difficult and what things could you do to overcome any hurdles?
5. What are some of the reasons people avoid seeing professionals? Are any of these reasons myths?

Reflection

Ask students to consider the last time they asked someone for help. Was it successful? If not, what could they have done to make it more successful?

Individual instruction and homework activities

If you have not already handed out the tipsheet, prior to beginning the following activities, provide each young person with the tipsheet on page 97. Allow sufficient time for this to be read and discussed.

Activity 5.1: Reaching out to others

A. Think about all the people and services you can turn to for support.

List five people to whom you could turn for help, advice or friendship. Write the name of a person you could talk to if you had any worries or concerns on each finger.

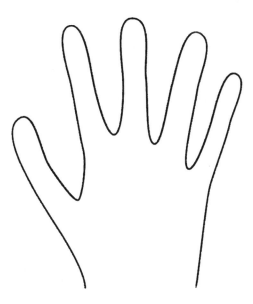

What might be the benefit of reaching out to others if you have a problem or concern?

Think of a situation in which you (or someone else) might use the following coping strategies to enlist the help of others:

- ❀ Social support
- ❀ Close friend
- ❀ Belonging to a group

Now, think of a situation when you (or someone else) might use:

- ❀ Social action
- ❀ Spiritual support
- ❀ Professional help

B. What might be some of the advantages of using a professional helper if you have a problem?

Activity 5.2: Seek out a professional

A. What are some other issues you could see a professional to talk about?

B. Now, think about people or agencies you could turn to for help and advice. Include people from your home, school and community. As well as people who have helped in the past, think about people/groups to whom you may not have turned before.

Write down the people or agencies you came up with.

Modifying the activities for students with additional needs

As this activity is about seeking help, it might be useful to ensure that students with additional needs understand some basic concepts related to help seeking before tackling the contents in this module:

❀ Is the individual with additional needs *able* to ask for help?

❀ Is the individual comfortable with asking for help?

❀ Is help easily accessible for the individual? E.g. in rural settings

❀ Can the person use alternative resources such as the internet and telephone?

❀ Does the individual have a basic understanding of those situations that might require help from another person?

The above suggestions are not only questions to consider, but a starting place for introducing the topic of help seeking to a student with additional needs.

Resources

These can be photocopied from the following pages
or downloaded from http://education.frydenberg.continuumbooks.com

Sometimes problems can seem too awful to talk about. Sometimes they might seem too minor or silly to bother other people with. Sometimes we might not be comfortable approaching someone else with a problem.

There are various people to turn to when problems arise or when you need to talk things through:

- ❀ *Friends* can be great support. Some concerns you may share with your friends include when you have had a fight with someone or are not getting along well with your brother or sister.
- ❀ *Teachers* can also help. You may turn to a teacher when you are having difficulties at school. For example, if you are being bullied or having trouble with your schoolwork.
- ❀ *Family members* can help too. Depending on what you want to talk about, you may choose to turn to your mum or dad, brother or sister, aunt or uncle or a grandparent.
- ❀ If the problem is something that you feel embarrassed or guilty about – or you simply don't want to talk about it with family or friends – there is another option: *professional help*.

Who are professionals?

Professionals are people whose job it is to assist other people with problems or issues – no matter how big or small. Some reasons for seeking out a professional are: 'I feel lonely', 'Sometimes I feel depressed', 'I find it hard to handle school work', 'Other kids are hassling me' or 'I'm unhappy at home'.

Professionals include doctors, school counsellors, psychologists, school chaplains, teachers and welfare coordinators.

Doctors: General practitioners (GPs) or family medical practitioners generally deal with illnesses or physical conditions. They can also be a helpful starting point if you have a problem with thoughts or feelings as they can point you in the right direction if they can't offer assistance.

Teachers: The primary role of the teacher is to teach or educate students, however teachers also have a responsibility to look out for students' welfare. Teachers can be a great place to turn if you have a concern because they know you and see you regularly. If they cannot assist you they will help you find appropriate help for your concern.

Psychologists/counsellors: A psychologist can help you deal with worries or concerns usually through talking, relaxation or assisting you to develop a plan of action to cope with or overcome the difficulty. Psychologists will keep your concern confidential unless it involves illegal activities or the harming of yourself or others. They can also help in areas such as career or educational testing and planning. Some schools have psychologists or counsellors on staff or who visit regularly. Other places they can be found include community centres, hospitals, health clinics and private practice

Welfare coordinators: Welfare coordinators deal with issues concerning the welfare of the students at the school – this includes where you live, your financial situation, problems at home, problems that affect your school attendance or performance as well as discipline issues and any other concerns that students may raise. They may offer counselling, advice, assistance applying for housing or financial support and a great many other practical ways to help. Because they are at the school, they can follow up and check with you to see how things are going.

School chaplains: Offer support in much the same way as welfare or youth workers. They give support, take care of needs and can often influence change within the school system.

Telephone help lines: These help lines or 'crisis lines' are set up so that someone is available to assist people in need over the phone – many of them are 24-hour lines. You can talk to someone about what is troubling you and they can offer you advice about what you should do, who you can contact, what your rights are etc. or just an ear to listen if that is what you want. You can remain anonymous. One problem is that because the services are so popular it can be difficult to get through. Keep trying or try another help line.

Where? Find listings in the telephone book, Yellow Pages or online.

Cost? Cost of a local call; some lines are free calls.

How do you contact a professional in a crisis?

If you, or someone you care about is in crisis, and you feel immediate action needs to be taken, you can contact the services listed below and they will be able to assist you.

- ❀ Emergency appointment with your GP. Check the telephone book or online for the phone number
- ❀ Call the local Crisis Assessment and Treatment (CAT) team.Check the phone book for the phone number
- ❀ Accident and Emergency department of your local hospital
- ❀ Ambulance: dial 999
- ❀ Support Line: dial 0208 554 9004
- ❀ Hope Line UK (suicide help): dial 0800 068 41 41
- ❀ Child Line free call 0800 1111
- ❀ Youth2Youth Helpline 0208 896 3675
- ❀ If you are at school you could also approach a trusted teacher or the welfare coordinator
- ❀ NSPCC Helpline: dial 0808 800 5000. The NSPCC Helpline is committed to a service to anyone who needs advice, help or information about concerns for a child's welfare, or to those who want to report concerns they have about a child or young person at risk of abuse.

Helpful websites

Child and Adolescent Mental Health Service (CAMHS) Consultants
www.camhsconsultants.co.uk/
CAMHS Consultants is an independent team of consultants with specialist expertise in services for children and young people who have emotional, behavioural and mental health problems.

Get Connected
www.getconnected.org.uk/
Get Connected can be reached by phone, email or webchat. They're designed to provide support and advice to young people with a range of problems.

D-2K
www.d-2k.co.uk/
Get the lowdown on how drugs affect your body, plus support and advice.

Kidscape
www.kidscape.org.uk/
Kidscape is a charity established specifically to prevent bullying and child sexual abuse. They run confidence building programmes for young people who have been bullied.

Young Minds
www.youngminds.org.uk/young-people
YoungMinds website offers information to young people about mental health and emotional wellbeing.

Bursting the Bubble
www.burstingthebubble.com
A website for teenagers who live in homes where there is domestic violence or where they are subjected to physical, sexual or emotional abuse.

Coping quiz

1. Give two reasons why young people may not seek help.
2. Name four professionals that you could seek help from in the community.
3. True or false: confidentiality means that the person you tell something to will not tell somebody else.

Further reading

Bailey, R. (1991), *50 Activities for Managing Stress*. Aldershot: Gower.
Synner, R. & Cleese, J. (1983), *Families and How to Survive Them*. London: Methuen.
Totman, R. (1990), *Mind, Stress, and Health*. London: Souvenir Press.

Module 6 – Coping with conflict

'Peace is not the absence of conflict, but the ability to cope with it.'

Anonymous

Contents

Learning cutcomes

The aim of this module is to explore conflict in life and utilize conflict resolution strategies. By the end of this module students will be able to identify the six steps involved in conflict resolution, as well as various positive strategies to manage anger.

In this session students will:

❀ Explore everyday scenarios that may be a source of conflict
❀ Learn various strategies to cope with conflict
❀ Be introduced to the topic of anger management

Instructor's notes

Mid to late adolescence is often accompanied by friendship changes and issues related to conflict. Conflict may arise from a variety of sources and commonly extends into the school and home environment. Because conflict is a common occurrence in typical relationships, conflict resolution skills are fundamental to maintaining healthy and happy relationships with people. Young people with poor conflict resolution skills are likely to experience increased aggression, social isolation, depression, feelings of loneliness and anxiety (James & Owens, 2004). Ongoing conflict can have a negative effect on the relationships of young people and be associated with low relationship satisfaction. This module aims to equip young people with the necessary skills to negotiate conflict which, after all, is an inevitable part of everyday life.

Setting the context

When we teach young people new concepts we need to ensure they can apply their new skills to situations beyond the learning context. The ability to generalize skills to wider social contexts is just as important as learning the skill itself. When it comes to conflict management and self-control the generalization of these skills is especially pertinent. While it may not be possible for instructors to practise new skills with students in real-life, social contexts, instructors can support the generalization of a new skill in the following ways:

1. Use real-life examples drawn from the students' own experiences
2. Use the language used by the young person wherever possible
3. Encourage students to reflect on how they apply the skill in real-life. Ask them questions such as:
   * Are there times or places when practising this new skill is particularly difficult for you?
   * Have you practised this skill in another context? How did you do?

Group and classwork activities

Ice breaker: Coping Frisbee

Time: 10 minutes

Materials: A Frisbee

Instructions: Ask students to sit in a circle. For this warm-up activity, ask students to throw the Frisbee around the circle. The person who catches the Frisbee has to name one thing they do when they feel angry. Draw students' attention to the variety of responses and explain that there are many ways of coping with anger. Some strategies may be helpful, while others may be less helpful.

Activity 1: Group discussion
Time: 15 minutes

Materials: None

Instructions: Gather the group in a large circle and discuss the following questions:

❀ Is conflict normal?
❀ If the conflict is between you and a friend or you and your peers (or a group), what could you do to resolve the conflict? (Answers could be peer mediation, seeing a counsellor, write a letter, taking time out.)
❀ Is enough ever enough? What should you do if you and a peer fight all the time?
❀ If the conflict is between you and a family member, what could you do? (Answers could be family mediation, family meeting, writing out the conflict resolution steps, counselling, taking time out, writing a letter.)

Activity 2: Alternatives to anger
Time: 40 minutes

Materials: Anger-inducing Scenario Cards (see page 108), whiteboard, whiteboard markers

Instructions: Using the whiteboard, ask students to brainstorm positive strategies to engage in when they are angry. These might include:

❀ Walk away
❀ Have some deep breaths
❀ Use assertive communication
❀ Talk to a friend
❀ Calm down

 Provide students with the tipsheet Hot Tip Number 6: Coping with Conflict (see page 110) and discuss the conflict resolution steps.

1. Understand *their* needs and concerns
2. Communicate *your* needs and concerns
3. Handle those emotions!
4. Brainstorm creative options
5. Consider your alternatives
6. Build win–win solutions

Suggest that these steps are another way in which individuals may manage anger.

Divide students into small groups and provide each group with an Anger-inducing Scenario Card. Ask students to role-play effective and non-effective ways of resolving the conflict. Once students have been provided with enough time to role-play the scenarios, gather the students in one large group again and ask each group to role-play the effective resolution to the conflict.

Summarize with the students what has been discussed. You might like to use the following script:

When you and someone in your life are in conflict, neither of you is feeling good. Both of you are feeling misunderstood and the problem is that, when we feel angry at someone, we stop listening and our defences go up.

The same skills you learnt for problem-solving can be modified to deal with conflict situations. The trick is to combine these with assertive communication. Together, effective problem-solving and assertive communication are very useful!

Activity 3: Relaxation guided imagery
Time: 10 minutes

Materials: None

Instructions: Ensure students are in a comfortable position. Read the following script:

Ensure you are lying or sitting in a comfortable position. Become aware of the sounds around you and begin to focus on your breath. Breathe deeply and slowly, paying close attention to the sound of your breath as your breathing slows down and your body relaxes. Notice your body and be aware of any stress or tight muscles. Begin releasing any tension you notice with each breath you exhale. Feel each breath massage your tension and exhale the tension from your body.

Next, I want you to think of a quiet and safe place. This can be a place where you feel safe and secure. Places you might choose may be under a tree in a green and leafy park. You might choose to lie on the soft sands of the beach. Your special place might be a favourite cosy place in your house or somebody else's house. Find a place that you love. Somewhere you can relax. Keep the picture of the special place in your mind. What does it look like on this day? Is it dark or light? Can you feel the warmth of this special place? What textures can you see and feel? What aromas can you smell?

I want you to imagine lying down in your special place. I want you to be able to feel your body melt into the floor or ground. You are relaxed in your special place and your body is letting go of the day. Your body is letting go of your thoughts and relaxing in the special place. You can feel each muscle letting go. Your toes, your feet, your calves, your thighs, your buttocks, your back and stomach, your chest and arms, your hands, your neck and your face. All your muscles are letting go.

Now turn your attention to the sounds of your special place. If you are at a beach, can you hear the waves of the ocean? Or, if you are in a park, can you hear birds? Let the gentle sounds relax you even further. Your special place is letting you unwind, take a deep breath and let go. Let your body let go and relax…

Turn your attention to the surface on which you are lying. Is it soft? Can you feel your body melting into it? With each deep breath your body lets go even more. Have some time to relax now and enjoy your special place…

When you're ready, allow yourself to slowly open your eyes and bring your attention back to the sounds of the room. Slowly move your arms and legs as you get sensation back into your muscles. Take a few seconds to sit up slowly.

Guided imagery is one way in which we can regulate the negative feelings associated with conflict. If you found this activity useful, you might like to consider trying it next time you feel the need to relax or have some quiet time.

Other relaxation activities that students may find useful include meditation, mindfulness, creating a mandala, guided relaxation, progressive muscle relaxation and deep breathing. Details of these activities may be found in the Further Reading section on page 110.

Reflection

Ask students to consider when they were last involved in a matter of conflict. Did they handle the situation effectively or not effectively? What would they do differently if the conflict arose again?

Individual instruction and homework activities

 If not already done, prior to beginning the following activities, provide each young person with the tipsheet Hot Tip Number 6: Coping with Conflict found on page 110. Allow sufficient time for this to be read and discussed.

Activity 6.1: Conflict reduction

You can reduce the amount of conflict in your life!
   Think about it:

On a scale of 1–10, how much conflict is there in your life? Circle a number.

1	2	3	4	5	6	7	8	9	1 0

How much conflict is there in your family? Tick your answer.

☐ Lots   ☐ Some   ☐ Not much   ☐ None

Who do you fight/argue with?

1.

2.

3.

What are the arguments normally about?

How do you feel after an argument?

If you had a magic wand and could make it so that you never had arguments with those three people ever again, what would it feel like? What would it mean for you?

Who feels good when they are in a conflict situation? No-one!

Activity 6.2: Taming anger

Anger is a natural emotion. It is one of four major emotions:

❀ Happiness
❀ Sadness
❀ Fear
❀ Anger

Anger is normal, and we all feel angry from time to time. It is how we DEAL with anger that causes trouble in our lives.

What does anger mean to you?

What makes you angry?

Responding to the emotion of anger with aggression is not helpful, but is nevertheless a common response.

Aggressive ways of dealing with anger include:

What happens when you respond to anger with aggression?

Consider the following questions:

How do you know you are getting angry?
Where do you feel anger in your body?
How could someone tell that you were getting angry?

Now we are going to think about some more helpful ways of responding and taming your anger because YOU can LEARN to TAME YOUR ANGER.

One of anger's key triggers is feeling *misunderstood*. You have the power to make yourself heard by assertive communication!

What are some strategies you can put in place when you feel your anger rising?

What calms you down?

What would be the benefit for you and your relationships if you learnt to control your anger?

Sometimes, rather than waiting for other people to change, for situations to improve or relationships to become more positive, we have to look within ourselves. You have the ability to make positive change in your life. You can control your feelings. You can control how you react to people. You can learn how to deal with your anger in more productive ways than with harsh words, aggression and physical force.

Modifying the activities for students with additional needs

Students with additional needs often require visual materials to describe how they are feeling. Use the Angry Body Scan on page 109 as well as the Emotion Meter from Module 2 (see page 61) to discuss the emotion of anger in regards to:

* Possible triggers likely to cause feelings of anger
* The various degrees of anger (e.g., very angry vs a little bit angry) and the relationship between different situations
* The various ways of coping with anger as well as regulation and relaxation strategies

You may need to list clear strategies for dealing with anger. Alternatively the students could devise some themselves. They may include:

* Have ten deep breaths
* Walk away from the conflict
* Find someone to talk to
* Practise other favoured relaxation activities
* Complete a quiet task (such as drawing or reading)
* Do something you enjoy
* Focus on the positive
* Spend some time with a close friend

It is always useful to think of *real-life* examples when discussing an emotion like anger, although any intervention should be performed when the student is in a relaxed and calm state. To further consolidate the topic of coping with conflict, use strategies such as role-play, social stories™ (Gray, 1995) and behaviour contracts to consolidate this topic.

Resources

These can be photocopied from the following pages
or downloaded from http://education.frydenberg.continuumbooks.com

Anger-inducing scenario cards

Photocopy the following cards and cut out for use in Activity 2 on page 102.

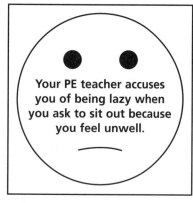

Your PE teacher accuses you of being lazy when you ask to sit out because you feel unwell.

Your parents will not let you go to your friend's party at the weekend.

You suspect a boy in another class has stolen your MP3 player.

Free Choice: Create your own scenario of something that could create conflict.

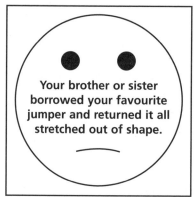

Your brother or sister borrowed your favourite jumper and returned it all stretched out of shape.

Free Choice: Create your own scenario of something that could create conflict.

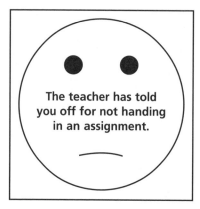

The teacher has told you off for not handing in an assignment.

Your best friend at school has not invited you over to her house at the weekend but invited another friend.

Angry body scan

Where do you feel anger in your body?

Tipsheet: Hot tip number 6: Coping with conflict

Conflict is 'people fighting against each other'.

A certain amount of conflict is normal. Each of us is an individual with our own needs and wants, which may sometimes clash with others'. Conflict in small amounts can even be good for relationships if the conflict is resolved well, with win–win outcomes. When conflict is ongoing, severe or occurring regularly it can lead to negative outcomes, such as aggression (words and actions) and sadness (depression). Our relationships suffer.

The differences between needs and wants.[2]

Conflict resolution: the steps
When you are in conflict with someone else:

1. Understand their needs and concerns
2. Communicate your needs and concerns
3. Handle those emotions!
4. Brainstorm creative options
5. Consider your alternatives
6. Build win–win solutions

What if the people around you are used to conflict? What if they do not know the steps?

❀ Be assertive
❀ Try to come at it from their point of view
❀ Offer to teach them the skills

Remember, at the end of the day, you cannot control other people. You can control your actions. You will feel better and respect yourself more for not responding with aggression and, instead, being assertive.

Coping quiz

1. Name four effective strategies that someone may use to assist anger.
2. True or false: conflict should be avoided. It is not normal for people to be involved in conflict.
3. What are the differences between needs and wants?
4. What are the six steps of conflict resolution?

Further reading

Adams, J. D. (1980), *Understanding and Managing Stress: A Book of Readings.* San Diego: University Associates.
Larkins, G. & Frydenberg, E. (2004), 'Two Types of Aggression and The Relationship with Coping: Implications for Educational Practice.' In *Thriving, Surviving or Going Under: Coping with Everyday Lives.* In 'Research on Stress and Coping in Education'. Greenwich: Information Age Publishing.
Powell, T. (2000), *Stress Free Living.* London: Dorling Kindersley.

Module 7 – Problem-solving

'Coping means that thing is very hard, difficult for you. But you also need to solve it.'

Li, 17

Contents

Learning outcomes

The aim of this module is to introduce students to the six-step problem-solving model. By the end of this module students will be able to apply the six-step model towards a range of issues and problems pertinent to their own experiences. The six steps that students will use are:

1. Define needs
2. Brainstorm solutions
3. Evaluate solutions
4. Choose solution
5. Plan and take action
6. Check results

In this session students will:

❀ Practise solving issues and dilemmas with scenarios related to their own personal experiences

❀ Assist peers in helping to solve a problem

❀ Expand skills in effective communication and help-seeking

Instructor's notes

We know that coping matters but we also know that one of the key resources for young people are the skills to deal with problems. Problem-solving is one of the most valuable skills that one can have with which to traverse everyday life. We know that there is a set of procedures that can be learnt. From work with adults, and more recently with adolescents, we know that those who believe that they are more effective problem-solvers are more likely to do well and be generally productive copers. Therefore we want not only to teach the skills but we want young people to feel that they are able to utilize the skills and to see themselves as effective in the way that they deal with problems.

We are likely to use problem-solving strategies in situations that we see as controllable. At the same time, when there is a situation that seems out of one's control (such as the separation of one's parents), problem-solving strategies are still required to manage the hassles relating to one's life, such as perhaps how to deal with moving between two households. Other problems might relate to finding a holiday job, getting to school on time, having the right books and equipment for each class, and so on.

Problem-solving involves the ability to plan, organize, take action, evaluate, adopt and summarize. It is a coping resource individuals can use when encountering stress, as poor problem-solving abilities may lead to ignoring or retreating from problems (Largo-Wight et al., 2005). Problem-solving is an essential component of one's coping repertoire. Indeed, it has often been considered to be part of proactive coping in that it is about anticipating and planning as well reacting in a systematic way to situations that present themselves.

Young people are faced with a variety of problems on a day to day basis. These problems may occur in a variety of contexts for a variety of reasons. Some problems are uncomplicated, that is, we solve them with ease and often without realizing. Other problems present greater challenges and often require the engagement of greater resources and considered thought.

Interestingly, *Webster's Dictionary* defines a problem as 'a question raised for inquiry, consideration, or solution'. This definition may run contrary to some young people's perceptions of problems as aversive or negative experiences. The benefits of teaching problem-solving to students are manifold. It helps both to normalize some of the problems experienced by young people and to reduce their negative perceptions of these problems. In addition it assists with reframing the perception of problems as inconveniences into the idea that they are challenges or dilemmas to be solved. Problem-solving is an essential component of effective coping. The way young people approach a problem determines how well they cope with the issue they are faced with. When young people can engage in effective problem-solving and use positive proactive reasoning skills, they are more likely to demonstrate a better ability to cope with the setbacks of everyday life.

Setting the context

The young people you work with will come from all walks of life. They will approach ideas and discussions from their own perspectives. All are shaped by prior experiences, cultural background, family and peer group influences. You may find that not all activities will suit the circumstances of the student or students with whom you are working. In order to respect the needs of individual students you may need to modify and adapt activities to recognize the diversity of the student body.

This module requires that students reflect upon the relationships and communication styles that inform their lives. Sometimes this may stir unpleasant memories or distress students with echoes of issues with which they are currently trying to cope. It is important to inform students that some of the information shared in a group setting may cause them discomfort. Students should thus be permitted to stop the discussion and continue elsewhere or, in extreme circumstances, to leave the room (providing they let an adult know where they are going) if they feel upset, uncomfortable or distressed by the topics explored in the session. It is also useful to remind students of the help they can access after the session should they need to discuss an issue with, for example, the school psychologist, school counsellor or a teacher.

Group and classwork activities

Ice breaker: Coping finders
Time: 10 minutes

Materials: Each student will need one A4-sized piece of paper and something to draw with. You will also need sticky tape.

Instructions: Each student uses the paper provided to draw a picture of himself or herself engaging in the coping strategy they use the most. Once the picture is completed, ask students to tape the pictures to their backs. Ask the student group to spend 3 minutes walking around the group studying each other's pictures. After 3 minutes, collect each picture and place them in the middle of the circle. Ask students to take turns looking at each picture to see if they can recall to whom the picture belongs.

Activity 1: Solution storm
Time: 15 minutes

Materials: Solution Storm Clouds (see page 125), whiteboard

Instructions: The purpose of this activity is to demonstrate to students how many solutions there may be to one particular issue or problem. Divide students into small groups or teams. If you are already working with a small group (that is, fewer than six children), this activity may be completed individually. Once students are formed into teams, ask them to come up with a team name. Record these names on a whiteboard.

To provide a brief overview of the activity, you might like to use the following script:

> We are going to play a game today that will demonstrate just how many solutions there may be to any given problem. Shortly I will read out a scenario. In your teams I want you to brainstorm as many solutions as possible to the problem and record each one on a cloud. The team with the most clouds is the winner. To give you a brief example, let's go through one together: Sally is walking along the beach and finds a wallet on the ground. She would love to keep it, but knows it might be the wrong thing to do, especially if she gets caught. What solutions can we come up with?

Collect enough responses from students to demonstrate that there are endless solutions to this problem. Some responses might be:

❀ Take the wallet to the police station
❀ Return the wallet to the closest shop
❀ Give the wallet to parents
❀ Throw the wallet in the sea
❀ Take money out of the wallet and put the wallet in the bin
❀ Look at the driver's licence and return the wallet to its owner

Read the following scenario out to students:

> Jenny has just logged onto the internet only to discover that someone has sent her another anonymous email saying how much they dislike her. She has received three this week and suspects that Sally and her friends are the ones sending the messages. Jenny is really upset.

Students may begin completing clouds. Allow them 10 minutes to complete the activity.

Once the clouds are completed, ask each group to read out their responses and tally the clouds for each group.

You might like to use the following prompt questions:

1. Were there more solutions to this problem than you initially suspected?
2. Did you generate more ideas as a team than you think you would have individually?

Activity 2: Choose your own ending
Time: 25 minutes

Materials: The tipsheet titled Hot Tip Number 7: Problem-solving (see page 126)

Instructions: Provide students with the tipsheet. Discuss the six-step problem-solving model.

1. *Define needs*: We all have basic needs that must be met in order to live. Some of these needs include: feeling safe, secure, sheltered and fed. The first step in problem-solving is to identify which of these needs is being violated. For example, is 'feeling respected' a valid need? How about the need to feel listened to or valued? Know the difference between needs and wants.[2]

2. *Brainstorm solutions*: The second phase to problem-solving is to brainstorm possible solutions. All possible solutions may be considered, no matter how silly they may seem at the time.

3. *Evaluate solutions*: Evaluate each of the solutions in light of their possible outcomes and consequences. Consider how the solution may affect yourself as well as the people around you.

4. *Choose solution*: Choose a solution based on the best possible outcome.

5. *Plan and take action*: Take steps to work out how to put your solution into practice. What responsibilities do you or others have? When will you begin to implement your solution?

6. *Check results*: Evaluate whether your solution worked. Have your needs been met? What has the outcome been for you and others around you? Do you need to choose another solution?

Students should be seated in a circle. Read out a scenario to students from the list below. In pairs, students take turns to act out alternative endings to the scenarios in front of the other students and practise as a group each of the six steps of problem-solving. Emphasize just how many alternative endings there can be to any given problem. Ask students to pick the most desired outcome. Possible scenarios to consider:

- You are getting ready to go to school. Upon opening the fridge you realize that your little sister has just used the last drop of milk. You were planning to have milk on your cereal.
- It is lunch time at school and you have realized that you left your lunch at home. You know that you will be catching the bus after school and may not eat until you get home which will be late.
- You have an assignment due tomorrow and you have not started it. You have had the assignment for four weeks and have been unsure about where to begin. The topic of the assignment seems too hard.
- You have a best friend in your class and you usually speak to her on the phone every night. Lately, your friend has not been returning your calls. You suspect your best friend is upset with you, but you don't know why. You have not spoken for five days and she has not been attending school.
- Your parents have always advised you not to take your wallet to school. One lunch time, you notice that your wallet is missing. You last saw it in your locker in the morning. You know your parents will be extremely upset when you tell them.
- A boy from school wants to drive you home after a party. You suspect he has been drinking and/or will be a reckless 'show-off' driver. You initially tell him that you don't want to drive with him, but you have not yet found another way to get home. He promises you he will drive carefully and slowly.

Activity 3: Help a friend

Time: 25 minutes

Materials: The tipsheet titled Hot Tip Number 7: Problem-solving on page 126

Instructions: Ask students to form pairs and decide which member of the pair will be known as A and which will be B. Once this is decided, ask student A to come up with a problem to share with student B. Instruct all student Bs to help student As solve their problem, using the six-step problem-solving model outlined in the tipsheet. Allow students 10 minutes to complete this activity then ask them to stop so that student A can assist student B with a problem. Students may wish to either use problems that they are currently dealing with or to make one up.

Close this activity by reminding students of the external resources they can access should they have a significant worry or concern.

Reflection

Ask students to think of a time when they were faced with a problem that was not solved effectively. How would the six-step problem-solving model have helped? How would such a model have lead to a different outcome? Give students the opportunity to share their thoughts if they are comfortable doing so.

Individual instruction and homework activities

This section lists activities that students can complete independently or with the guidance of another person.

If not already handed out, prior to beginning the following activities, provide each young person with the tipsheet Hot Tip Number 7: Problem-solving found on page 126. Allow sufficient time for this to be read.

Activity 7.1: Solving problems

Let's put the six steps of problem-solving (see page 115) into practice for the following situations:

Situation 1: Jasmine and Anna are going to a school dance on Friday night. They both went shopping together two nights before the dance and found a gorgeous dress. Both girls desperately want the same dress. Jasmine is happy for them to both to wear the same dress, but Anna has told Jasmine that she will not go to the dance if they are wearing the same thing. If you were Jasmine, how could you look at this problem?

Step 1. What needs does this scenario encompass? (e.g., need to feel listened to, need to feel safe, etc):

_____

Step 2. Brainstorm solutions to the problem by listing all the options you have:

_____

Step 3. Evaluate the solutions (e.g., how will it affect you and the people around you? What are the consequences of each solution?)

_____

Step 4. Choose the best option that is a 'win–win' for everyone:

_____

Step 5. Plan and take action:

_____

What has to be done?

_____

Who is to do it?

Activity 7.1: Solving problems – continued

When will it be done?

_____

Step 6. Check how well you did in solving the problem. Was the solution successful? What could be the positive outcomes of your plan?

_____

If your plan does not work, how could you improve any parts of the process?

_____

Situation 2: It is Sunday and Gina has an art assignment due on Monday that she has not started. Gina's best friend, Justine, has asked her to go to the beach. It is warm and sunny and Gina is worried that Justine will not want to be her friend if she keeps turning down invitations to hang out on the weekend.

Step 1. What needs are covered in this scenario? (e.g., need to feel listened to, need to feel safe, etc.):

_____

Step 2. Brainstorm solutions to the problem by listing all the options you have:

_____

Step 3. Evaluate the solutions (e.g., How will it affect you and the people around you? What are the consequences to each solution?)

_____

Step 4. Choose the best option that is a 'win–win' for everyone:

_____

Step 5. Plan and take action:

_____

What has to be done?

_____

Who is to do it?

_____

When will it be done?

_____

Step 6. Check how well you did in solving the problem. Was the solution successful? What could be the positive outcomes of your plan?

_____

If your plan does not work, how could you improve any parts of the process?

_____

Activity 7.1: Solving problems – continued

Situation 3: Simon knows that the school has a policy forbidding the use of MP3 players. He has ignored the rule this year and today he discovers that his MP3 player is missing from his bag. He suspects it has been stolen.

_____

Step 1. What needs does this scenario involve? (e.g., need to feel listened to, need to feel safe, etc.):

_____

Step 2. Brainstorm solutions to the problem by listing all the options you have:

_____

Step 3. Evaluate the solutions (e.g., How will it affect you and the people around you? What are the consequences to each solution?)

_____

Step 4. Choose the best option that is a 'win–win' for everyone:

_____

Activity 7.1: Solving problems – continued

Step 5. Plan and take action:

_____

What has to be done?

_____

Who is to do it?

_____

When will it be done?

_____

Step 6. Check how well you did in solving the problem. Was the solution successful? What could be the positive outcomes of your plan?

_____

If your plan does not work, how could you improve any parts of the process?

_____

Activity 7.2: Remember the steps

To ensure that you are able to use the six-step problem-solving model in all situations, it is essential that you can recall each of the six steps. Here are some simple activities that will help you remember:

Exposure: look, cover, write, check

LOOK and COVER	WRITE and CHECK
1. Define needs	
2. Brainstorm solutions	
3. Evaluate solutions	
4. Choose solution	
5. Plan and take action	
6. Check results	

Rehearsal: put the following steps in order

Evaluate solutions, Check results, Plan and take action, Brainstorm solutions, Define needs, Choose solution.

1 _____   2 _____   3 _____

4 _____   5 _____   6 _____

Create a mnemonic

Sometimes when we need to remember a list of words, we can do so easily by taking the first letter of each word to make up a wacky sentence, poem or short story. For example:

1. **Define needs**
2. **Brainstorm solutions**
3. **Evaluate solutions**
4. **Choose Solution**
5. **Plan and take action**
6. **Check results**

Dull **B**oys **E**at **C**hocolate **P**ancakes **C**arefully.

Your turn: D _____

B _____

E _____

C _____

P _____

C _____

Modifying the activities for students with additional needs

A shortened version of the problem-solving model may be used for students with additional needs:

State the problem: What is the problem?

Think of all possible solutions: The second phase to problem-solving is to think about all the possible solutions. All solutions may be considered, no matter how silly they may seem at the time.

Look at each solution: Think about what may happen after each solution. What would happen to you? What would happen to others?

Choose solution: Choose a solution based on the best possible outcome.

Check results: Check to see whether your solution worked. Have your needs been met? What has the outcome been for you and others around you? Do you need to choose another solution

When working with children with additional needs, it may be better to draw on problems taken directly from their own experiences. You might like to practise solving these problems using the following template:

Step 1. Say what the problem is:

Step 2. Brainstorm ways of solving the problem by listing all the options you have:

Step 3. Look at each solution. What are the consequences of each alternative?

Step 4. Choose the best solution:

Step 5. Check how well you did in solving the problem. Did your solution work?

If your plan does not work, how could you improve any parts of the process?

Resources

These can be photocopied from the following pages
or downloaded from http://education.frydenberg.continuumbooks.com

Solution storm clouds

Photocopy and enlarge these clouds. Make sure you have plenty of clouds for students to use.

Tipsheet: Hot tip number 7: Problem-solving

___

One of the most positive and direct ways to cope with a problem is to *solve it!*

A simple problem solving approach can be applied to many (although not all) types of problems. If you use problem-solving effectively, it can save you a lot of time and stress – you may even be able to deal with issues *before* they turn into real problems. Problem-solving can work well either when considering individual problems or when used in a group conflict situation (where people have different and opposing ideas).

How to solve a problem[3]
To solve problems you will need to take the time to think carefully about the problem and use a step-by-step process. The six steps to problem-solving are:

1. *Define needs*: We all have basic needs that must be met in order to live. Some of these needs include: feeling safe, secure, sheltered and fed. The first step in problem-solving is to identify which of these needs is being violated. For example, is feeling respected a valid need? How about the need to feel listened to or valued?
2. *Brainstorm solutions*: The second phase to problem-solving is to brainstorm all possible solutions. All possible solutions may be considered no matter how silly they may seem at the time.
3. *Evaluate solutions*: Evaluate each of the solutions in light of their possible outcomes and consequences. Consider how the solution may affect yourself as well as the people around you.
4. *Choose solution*: Choose a solution based on the best possible outcome.
5. *Plan and take action*: Take steps to work out how to put your solution into practice. What responsibilities do you or others have? When will you begin to implement your solution?
6. *Check results*: Evaluate whether your solution worked. Have your needs been met? What has the outcome been for you and others around you? Do you need to choose another solution?

A guide to solving problems

When you have a problem that must be solved these are the steps that should be involved

1. Define needs

2. Brainstorm solutions

3. Evaluate solutions

4. Choose solution

5. Plan and take action

6. Check results

1. Define needs

My needs are:

2. Brainstorm ways of solving the problem

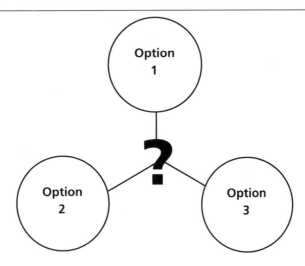

3. Evaluate the options

4. Choose the best option

The best option is:

5. Plan and take action

I am going to try this option out by or on:

6. Check out how well you did in solving the problem. What was the outcome? What would you do differently next time?

Coping quiz

1. Name the six steps to problem-solving.
2. How would you use the six steps to solve the following scenarios?
    a You slept in and have missed the bus for school.
    b You best friend has just told you that she thinks she has lost her dad's mobile phone which he lent her. How will you help her?

Further reading

Frydenberg, E. (2005), *Tough Minded and Tender Hearted: The Life and Work of Morto Deutsch*. Bowen Hills: Australian Academic Press.

Gordon, T. (1974), *Teacher Effectiveness Training*. New York: Peter H. Wyden.

Lewis, R & Frydenberg, E. (2007), 'When problem-solving is not perceived as effective: How do young people cope'. In *Emerging Thought and Research on Student, Teacher and Administrator Stress and Coping*. Volume in series on Stress and Coping in Education, Greenwich: Information Age Publishing.

Module 8 – Social problem-solving

'Coping is the ability to deal with situations and resolve problems that arise no matter how hard it may get.'

Angela, 16

Contents

Group and classwork activities

Individual instruction and homework activities

Resources

Learning outcomes

The aim of this module is to teach students the skills to deal with situations in relationships. By the end of this module students will be better equipped to handle and avoid teasing, rejection, friendship group changes, bullying and isolation.

In this session students will:

- Understand the important features of a relationship
- Identify the different levels to a relationship
- Reflect on the six-step problem-solving model and how this relates to social situations
- Prevent, avoid and manage social conflict and bullying

Instructor's notes

Friendship group changes and issues related to bullying, feelings of loneliness and social isolation commonly occur during adolescence. These events are often unavoidable and do not discriminate between school type, socio-economic status and level of family support. It could be argued that all young people will experience a negative event related to socialization at some point in their lives. Equipping young people with the necessary skills to develop positive relationships and to cope with negative social occurrences is critical in fostering resilience and a life-long ability to create and maintain effective relationships with others.

Setting the context

When discussing social-based conflict and negative social events, there is a natural inclination for young people to use the names of those whom they perceive to have done them wrong. While self-blame is not helpful, neither is it helpful to blame others and no names should be used in the session. When setting the context of this module talk about the important features of friendships and relationships such as trust and empathy.

Group and classwork activities

Ice breaker: Greeting
Time: 10 minutes

Materials: Written instructions, either on the board or given to each member of the group

Instructions: Give the group a set of tasks to complete, for instance find a person in the group who has a birthday in the same month as you (how do they celebrate?), who likes tennis (when and where do they play?), who has a dog (name and type?), who has a cat (name and type?) and ask each person to expand and ask questions as a conversation starter.

Activity 1: Understanding important features of relationships
Time: 10 minutes

Materials: None

Instructions: Identify engaging characteristics. The joy of friendship lies partly in the enjoyable things that friends do together, and partly in the positive verbal and non-verbal signals exchanged between friends. For example, people who smile at each other a lot are likely to be friends. Smiling is a powerful reinforcer and a sign of friendship. Smiling, eye contact, tone of voice, gaze, gestures, posture (direct and forward) and appearance are important (see also Module 4, Activity 1 on page 79).

Think of a time you were with a friend. What were the things that they did to make you enjoy spending time with them? What did you do? Discuss in pairs and share your experiences. Remember to focus on the positive.

Activity 2: Identify levels of relationships

Time: 10 minutes

Materials: Handout entitled Identify Levels of Relationships on page 136

Instructions: Provide students with the handout. There are different levels of relationships. For each level of relationship identify one individual in your circle at each level.

1. **Close** People you have known for some time, share stories, trust, share feelings

2. **Friends** People you spend time with at school and in other settings and go on occasional outings with

3. **Acquaintances** People you know from sports settings, school or clubs

4. **Familiar faces** People to whom you have not spoken but can identify by name or sight

5. **Strangers** People you do not know

Activity 3: Engaging in social relationships

Time: 10 minutes

Materials: None

Instructions: There are different levels of relationships. For each level of relationship there are conversational skills to be utilized. The basic social skill sequence has four steps: A makes an initial move, e.g. asks a question. B responds. If this is not what A wanted he makes a modified move, e.g. asks a more direct question. B may give a more helpful answer. There can be repeated cycles of utterances. Divide the group into pairs and ask them to identify who is A and who is B and engage in a conversation.

Important features of such conversations are: showing interest and being a good listener (see Module 4). Reverse roles and discuss what each person found helpful.

The activity can be extended so that the conversation takes a more elaborate form, e.g. A responds to B's reply, B asks a question about that, A responds and so on. For example:

A: How are you planning to spend the weekend?

B: I play in a tennis team and then it is my brother's birthday?

A: How does your family celebrate birthdays?

B: We usually have a small party with family. How does your family celebrate?

Activity 4: Features of friendships (optional)

Time: 5 minutes

Materials: None

Instructions: Friendships require loyalty, commitment, concern for the other's welfare and generally sharing of ideas and resources. They are also about give and take – or, more specifically, taking an interest in the other person. We've all met people who like to think the world revolves around them, for example, they turn the focus of conversations to themselves, always decide on group activities and need lots of attention. Friendships and relationships that aren't reciprocal are not likely to last – you'll get what you give!

Select two volunteers to role-play in front of the class. Have the students engage in a normal conversation but one student must act as the 'selfish friend'. The role of the 'selfish friend' is to turn the conversation back to themselves at all times. Allow the students to role-play for a minute or so.

Reflection

Ask the student volunteers to feedback to the class on what it was like to role-play each character. Ask the class to comment on what they noticed about the conversation. Have they met anyone like the 'selfish friend' before? What do they think might happen to the 'selfish friend' over time?

Individual instruction and homework activities

 Prior to beginning the following activities, provide each young person with the tipsheet Hot Tip Number 8: Social Problem-solving found on page 137. Allow sufficient time for this to be read and discussed.

Activity 8.1: Social problem-solving

Managing friendships can sometimes be challenging. As individuals we usually have a range of different interests (e.g. sport, music, art, etc). This can lead us to meet a lot of different people and develop different friendship groups. No-one wants to be friends with someone who lets them down and doesn't consider others' feelings. We can't always please everyone but we can always be mindful of others' feelings and have respect for those around us.

Situation: Someone new has joined your class. She has invited you to her party. Your regular friends also want you to go out with them on the same night. Use the six steps to problem-solving below to decide what you will do.

The six steps to problem-solving
1. Define needs
2. Brainstorm solutions
3. Evaluate solutions
4. Choose solution
5. Plan and take action
6. Check results

Teaching tip

Remind students of the six steps to solving problems from Module 7.

Activity 8.2: Bully resilience

If you asked a class of students to raise their hands if they've ever experienced bullying there's a strong chance that every student will raise a hand. Some young people experience bullying on a daily basis, to extreme levels, while others may only be able to recall one or two times when someone did or said something to them that made them feel upset or left out. Throughout life there will always be bullies, victims and bystanders. Everyone has the ability to choose how he or she will cope in such situations.

   Possible solutions for dealing with bullying are:

❀ Finding other friends
❀ Building confidence through sport, schoolwork, outside-school interests
❀ Using assertive communication

Take a walk in someone else's shoes

There's a student in your class who faces verbal abuse and name-calling on a daily basis. This happens everyday but no one ever does anything to help.

How would it feel to be the victim?

What could you do to solve the problem?

Modifying the activities for students with additional needs

The examples and situations outlined in this module need to be modified for groups of students who are at a different stage, for example early adolescence, late adolescence, boys-only class, girls-only class or ethnically different. For groups that are likely to be gifted and teased more frequently or have an Autism Spectrum Disorder, like Asperger's Syndrome (see Section 3), the time spent on social coping skills needs to be extended, as do the examples. Students should be encouraged to bring their own experiences into the session and asked what worked and what did not work.

Resources

These can be photocopied from the following pages or downloaded from http://education.frydenberg.continuumbooks.com

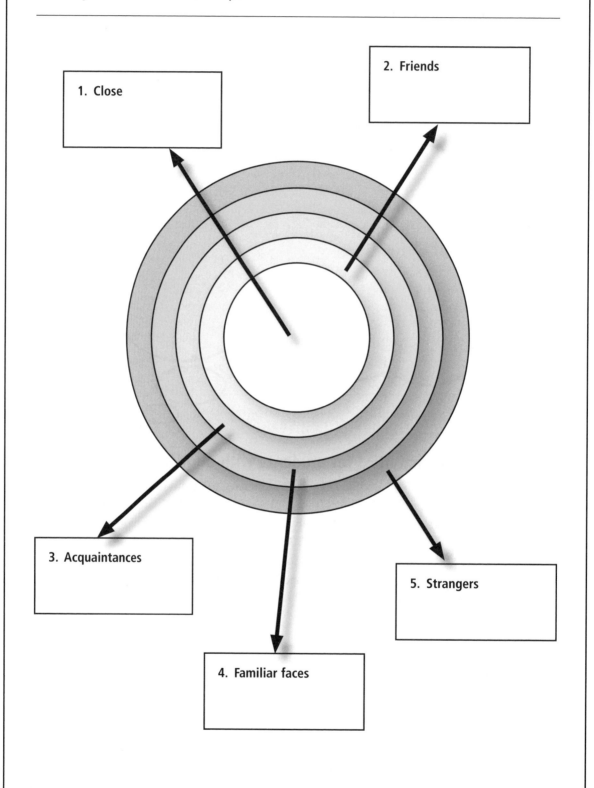

Identify levels of relationships

1. Close

2. Friends

3. Acquaintances

4. Familiar faces

5. Strangers

Tipsheet: Hot tip number 8: Social problem-solving

Being a young person is often a time where you may experience changes in your friendship circles as well as possible conflict from time to time. These situations can cause great difficulty for some people and some young people report feeling overwhelmed.

Like general problem-solving, problem-solving for a social situation uses the same six-step solution:

1. Define needs
2. Brainstorm solutions
3. Evaluate solutions
4. Choose solution
5. Plan and take action
6. Check results

Social problems in practice

1. Define needs and say what the problem is

Casey feels that her friendship with Jess has changed and she is not happy with it. Casey needs to feel like Jess is still her friend.

2. Brainstorm ways of solving the problem by listing options

❀ Casey could talk with her friend and tell her how she feels

❀ Casey could get advice from a school counsellor.

❀ Casey could spend more time with Jess in an effort to get things back on track.

3. Evaluate solutions

4. Choose the best option that is a 'win–win' for everyone

Communication. Casey could talk to her friend. She could have a heart-to-heart talk with Jess and tell her how she feels.

5. Plan and take action

What has to be done?

Casey needs to explain to Jess how she feels and that she has the right to have other friends as well, just as Jess does. Casey should tell Jess that she wants to get their friendship back to the way it used to be and that she is willing to make an effort, but that Jess has to try too.

❀ Who is to do it?

❀ When will it be done? At a time when Casey and Jess have some private time together.

6. Check results – how well you did in solving the problem

What are the positive outcomes of your plan?

Communication. Talking to her friend opens up the lines of communication and Casey can express how she really feels. Friends should be very open with each other.

Social problem-solving

Listen to everyone's feelings

❀ Teach others to listen by listening to them

❀ Think about how others are feeling

❀ Listen quietly and attentively

❀ Check with them that you have understood correctly

❀ Your feelings and theirs are important

❀ Tell them how you feel (without attacking them personally)

Solve problems peacefully

❀ Set aside time to talk about the problem

❀ Ask them how they see the problem

❀ State clearly how you see the problem

❀ Find out what everybody's needs and concerns are

❀ Together, think of as many solutions as you can

❀ Together, choose a combined solution that best meets everybody's needs. Then try it out!

❀ Check that the solution is working

Care about each other

❀ Have fun together

❀ Show others that you like them

❀ Make time to be together – share stories at meal-times, tell them about your day

❀ Tell them what you like about them

❀ Help them appreciate people who are different

❀ Talk about the world as the home of us all

Encourage co-operation

❀ When possible, make agreements instead of imposing your will

❀ Notice and praise others when they co-operate and help out

❀ If you do make a rule, explain why its important

❀ Set up consequences, consistently and reliably

❀ Hitting and yelling don't work – use peaceful alternatives

❀ Follow through on your promises

Coping quiz

1. List which of the 23 coping strategies are most helpful for the dealing with social situations.
2. List which of the 23 strategies would not be helpful in dealing with social situations.

Further reading

D'Zurilla, T. J., Nezu, A.M., & Maydeu-Olivares, A. (2002), *Social Problem-Solving Inventory-Revised (SPSI-R)*. North Tonawanda: Multi-Health Systems, Inc.

D'Zurilla, T.J., Nezu, A. M. & Maydeu-Olivares, A. (2004), 'What is social problem solving?: Meaning, models, and measures.' In E.C. Chang, T.J. D'Zurilla & L. Sanna, (eds) *Social Problem Solving: Theory, Research, and Training*, 11–27. Washington: American Psychological Association.

Module 9 – Decision-making

'Learning to cope is helpful, because when you're in difficult and stressful situations in your life you can decide to move on and go on with your life instead of stressing over things that could be fixed with coping skills.'

Claudia, 16

Contents

Learning outcomes

The aim of this module is to teach students how to make considered decisions through evaluating various alternatives to a given situation. By the end of this module students will be able to formulate various alternative options available when facing a decision and choose an appropriate outcome that will meet short-term and long-term goals and needs.

In this session students will:

❀ Be able to identify and create a variety of alternatives to a given situation that requires a decision

❀ Engage in a decision-making model

- ❀ Choose a decision that is considered and reflects short- and long-term goals
- ❀ Consider risky decisions – how big is the risk?
- ❀ Announce decisions
- ❀ Stick to decisions

Instructor's notes

Adolescence is a time of growing independence. Young people increasingly face a variety of choices and are often required to make decisions that can have long-term consequences. Decision-making is a coping skill that requires the individual to make a considered choice in light of goals and needs. The decisions may relate to short- or long-term goals. They may relate to major decisions or minor ones. The decisions may involve risks where the consequences are manageable and those where the consequences have too great a downside. Following a decision-making procedure, there are helpful strategies that relate to sticking to decisions, including being able to share the decision.

Setting the context

We all have to make decisions as part of everyday life but some of our decisions have more far-reaching consequences than do others. When we are stressed it is usually about feeling like there are too many options and not knowing where to begin. Making good decisions is a learnt skill. We need to know what our goals are, what the real problem is, how this decisional problem fits in with our goals and what are the options available. Then we can engage in the decisional process. Tell others about it, put it into action and find ways to stick to the decision but always review the outcome, just as one does in problem-solving. Have I tackled the correct problem? Is there another way of dealing with the situation? Can the decision be reversed? Do I have to frame the outcome in positive terms? I will take a different path to the same direction.

Group and classwork activities

Ice breaker: Decisions, decisions
Time: 10 minutes

Materials: None

Instructions: Ask students to stand in the middle of the room and ask them to move to either side of the room to indicate their preference of one of the words in the following pairs:

- ❀ Cheese or chocolate
- ❀ Milk or water
- ❀ Play or work
- ❀ Run or swim

* Read or write
* Eat or drink
* Caring or careless
* Friend or enemy
* Helpful or unhelpful
* Sad or happy
* Shower or bath

Each time a decision is made ask students to reflect on the choice they had made. Had they made a decision they were happy with? Did they consider their decision carefully? What was it like to make a decision so hastily without time for consideration? This activity may be modified according to the group. Word pairs could include personal attributes or coping skills.

Activity 1: Defining the decisional problem

Time: 10 minutes

Materials: Pencils and paper

Instructions: Inform students that you will read out a decisional problem that involves a number of people and a number of possible solutions. Ask them to write down the name of the person and the decision that has to be made on the piece of paper provided. Ask them to use the following setting out:

Name	Decision

Read the following:

Lena had promised her brother Tom, sister Amy and best friend Julia that she would go to the football match with them. She has just had her assignment returned by the teacher and has been told that she will have to do some more work on it before re-submitting it. Who are the people involved in making the decision?

Activity 2: Linking goals to decisions

Time: 10 minutes

Materials: Pencils and paper, whiteboard and markers

Instructions: Inform students that it is important to identify one's goals before one can decide how to make the decision. Explain that we each have goals and decisions that we have to follow in order to achieve them. Using the whiteboard, give students the following examples and request that they formulate their own goals and decisions on the paper provided:

Examples of goals	Examples of decisions
Get into the school debating team	Practise at home at meal-times
Learn to play the guitar	Research the cost and teacher
Get into the school athletics team	Go to the gym during lunch break
_____	_____
_____	_____
_____	_____

Activity 3: Minor decisions and major decisions

Time: 5 minutes

Materials: Whiteboard and markers

Instructions: Explain to students that some decisions are small and can be made quickly and some are large. Identifying the small decisions that can be made quickly and those with long-term consequences is sometimes not clear cut. On the whiteboard list the following decisions and ask the group to decide whether these are major or minor:

Decision	Major	Minor
Should I go to the movies tonight?	☐	☐
What subjects will I choose next year?	☐	☐
What shall I wear to my friend's party?	☐	☐
What project will I choose for my next assignment?	☐	☐

Activity 4: Risk-taking (optional)

Time: 5 minutes

Materials: Pencils and paper

Instructions: Ask students if they identify themselves as being risk-takers or more cautious people. Next, ask them to imagine there are three diving boards to choose from. Ask which one they would choose: the highest or the middle one or the lowest and why. Allow group discussion.

Ask students to think of a risky situation and share it with a partner. Once sitting in pairs, ask them to ask their partner the following questions:

❀ How risky was it on a scale of 1–10, with 10 being very risky?
❀ Why was it risky?
❀ What action did you choose?
❀ Would you have liked to have been more risky or less risky?

Ask each pair to record their responses on a piece of paper using the following headings and then discuss:

Risky situation   Why risky?

Reflection

Ask students to reflect on their goals, decisions that they have had to make and decisions that they will have to make, who is involved and whether they are minor or major.

Individual instruction and homework activities

Prior to beginning the following activities, provide each young person with the tipsheet Hot Tip Number 9: Decision-making found on page 152. Allow sufficient time for this to be read and discussed.

Activity 9.1: Decisions

Decisions often involve or impact others as well as yourself. Your goals are important, as are the likely benefits or downsides for both yourself and the other person(s). Consider all those aspects in the chart below.

A guide to decision-making

THE DECISION I MUST MAKE IS:

_____

Let's make it a GOOD decision!

1. Keep your goals in mind.

2. List your options *and*

3. Evaluate each one.

My goals are:

Options	Upsides		Downsides	
	For you	For others	For you	For others

Highlight the option you decide upon

4. Review your decision and its outcomes.

Are you happy with the decision you made? NO?

Then you may want to review your options. _____

Activity 9.2: Small and big decisions

A. Think of one small decision that you made recently.

_____

B. How did this help or hinder your goals?

_____

C. What other choices could have been made?

_____

D. How did you evaluate which choice was the best one to make?

_____

A. Think of a big decision you have made in the past year.

_____

B. How did this help or hinder your goals?

_____

C. What other choices could have been made?

_____

D. How did you evaluate which choice was the best one to make?

Activity 9.3: Making decisions

A. Have a go at making the following decision:

Situation: Your dad has asked if you would like to go away on a family holiday with him to Italy. You have wanted to go to Italy for a long time. Unfortunately your dad is leaving during the last week of term which is the same week that you have a very important English exam. You don't want to miss out on going to Italy, but you also know that the exam is very important. What should you do?

List your options:

Option 1

_____

Option 2

_____

Option 3

_____

What are the upsides (positives) for these options?

Upsides for option 1

_____

Upsides for option 2

_____

Upsides for option 3

_____

What are the downsides (negatives) for these options?

Downsides for option 1

_____

Downsides for option 2

_____

Downsides for option 3

Activity 9.3: Making decisions – continued

B. You have decided to take the option of negotiating with your English teacher to sit your exam early. Think about the following:

What are the consequences for yourself?

_____

What are the consequences for others?

_____

Remember, to make good decisions you need to:

1. Keep your **goals** in mind
2. Consider all of your choices (**options**)
3. Evaluate the **options** – the **upsides** and the **downsides** – for each choice
4. Review your decision and outcomes

C. Have a go at making the following decision:

Situation: Jenny would like to be in the school musical. She needs to audition for the part but is not sure that she can sing well enough.

List your options:

Option 1

_____

Option 2

_____

Option 3

_____

What are the upsides (positives) for these options?

Upsides for option 1

_____

Upsides for option 2

_____

Upsides for option 3

Activity 9.3: Making decisions – continued

What are the downsides (negatives) for these options?

Downsides for option 1

_____

Downsides for option 2

_____

Downsides for option 3

_____

What decision should Jenny make?

_____

D. Now have a go at making this decision:

Situation: You want to try skydiving because all your friends have tried it. This has been something that has never appealed to you in the past. Your friend John asks if you would like to join him skydiving on Sunday. You know that it is pretty costly.

List your options:

Option 1

_____

Option 2

_____

Option 3

_____

What are the upsides (positives) for these options?

Upsides for option 1

_____

Upsides for option 2

_____

Upsides for option 3

Activity 9.3: Making decisions – continued

What are the downsides (negatives) for these options?

Downsides for option 1

_____

Downsides for option 2

_____

Downsides for option 3

_____

What decision should you make?

_____

Sticking to decisions

There are two important elements that help us to stick to decisions. One is making your decision known. The high profile comedian who had made her reputation on being the jovial 'fat lady' needed to lose weight for health reasons. She announced it in a newspaper and was pictured on numerous occasions, looking better each time. This acted as a reinforcement for her to stick to her plan until she achieved her goal. Sticking to decisions is also helpful if you write down your decision, the date you made it and the date by which you have to report to yourself.

Did you stick to it or do you need to review and have a different plan of action. Remember no 'self-blame', rather use a positive self-statement, such as, 'I did my best but I might need to achieve that goal in a different way – smaller steps, perhaps more help, more time.' Maybe it is the goal that needs to be reviewed. Remember to 'focus on the positive'.

Modifying the activities for students with additional needs

For students with additional needs it is important to use language that is appropriate for their age and cognitive functioning. Some students may benefit from simplified language such as 'good and bad choices'. Work surrounding this topic may further be simplified by teaching basic cause and effect-type activities and brainstorming multiple situations, decisions and outcomes. Often repetition is the key to ensuring that scenarios are relevant to the individual student. Provide students with opportunities to practise their decision-making using real-life examples as well as role-play.

Resources

These can be photocopied from the following pages
or downloaded from http://education.frydenberg.continuumbooks.com

Tipsheet: Hot tip number 9: Decision-making

Making decisions is something that we all do every day. Some decisions are minor ones (such as, should I watch this movie or that movie?). Other decisions are more major and may impact on our goals, our success, our future and other people. As you move through and beyond secondary school, some of the decisions that you will need to make will be extremely important.

For example:_____

_____

We have all made many decisions in our lives: Some good, some not so good. What sort of decisions have you made or are you likely to make in the future?

_____

_____

To make good decisions, we need to consider several things:

❀ Goals
❀ Options
❀ Outcomes
❀ Review

First, keep your goals in mind. These will help you make choices.

Secondly, you need to consider all your choices.
What are your options? Sometimes there are so many options that it is confusing and difficult to weigh them up. Other times there are too few.

Thirdly, you need to evaluate the options.
Consider all the facts and possible outcomes that relate to each option. To make sure you don't forget anything, write this information down. What are the upsides and downsides (advantages and disadvantages/gains and losses) that might come with each option?
How will your choice affect others? What are the gains and losses for them?
It is important to consider how your choice will affect others, so that you can take this into account when making your decision.

Lastly, review your decision and outcomes.
You may need to re-think your choice, or if this is not possible, use positive-thinking and make the best of the choice you have made.

Recall the situation you were just supplied and the options you came up with.

Situation: You have been invited by your friends to go for a five-day summer camp next week. However, you had intended to spend the week practising tennis for the upcoming school competition. You don't want to miss out on the fun times camping with your friends, but you also know you need the tennis practice.

Here are some possible options that you may have thought of:

1. **Go on the camp**

   Upsides:
   - ❀ Have fun
   - ❀ Be with friends
   - ❀ Get more camping experience

   Downsides:
   - ❀ No time to practise tennis
   - ❀ Might not do well in the competition

2. **Don't go on the camp so you can practise tennis**

   Upsides:
   - ❀ Improve tennis skills
   - ❀ Increased chance of winning the competition

   Downsides:
   - ❀ Miss out on a fun time with friends

3. **Identify the best person to speak to (for example, the tennis coach or camp supervisor) and negotiate being able to practise tennis while at camp**

   Upsides:
   - ❀ Might be able to do both!
   - ❀ Have fun with friends
   - ❀ Improve tennis skills

   Downsides:
   - ❀ It might not be possible to do both. For example, there may not be anywhere to practise tennis while at camp

Now that you have learnt the process involved in making good decisions, its time to practise decision-making!

Making decisions is something that we all do every day, but it is worthwhile to take the time to really think about the decisions we are making, especially the more important ones. Sometimes, even when you have put time into making a decision, you will realize later on that you did not make the best choice. That's OK! You can only make decisions based on the information at hand – you cannot see into the future!

Coping quiz

1. What are some considerations we need to make when making a decision?
2. How do we evaluate whether we are going to make a good or bad decision?
3. Why is it important to consider goals when making a decision?

Further reading

Abelson, R., and A. Levi (1985), 'Decision making' in *Handbook of Social Psychology*, , G. Lindzey, G. and Aronson, E.(eds).New York: Random House, 231–309.

Arnett, J. (1992), 'Reckless behavior in adolescence: A developmental perspective' *Developmental Review*, 12, 339–373.

Baron, J., and R. Brown, (1991) (eds), *Teaching Decision Making to Adolescents*. Hilldale: Lawrence Erlbaum.

Bernard, M. E. (2006), *Cognitive Behavioural and Rational Emotive Approaches to Childhood Problems*. Participant Handout, Melbourne Graduate School of Education, The University of Melbourne.

Bernard, M. E. (1991), *Procrastinate Later: How to Motivate Yourself to Do It Now.* Melbourne: Schwartz & Wilkinson.

Module 10 – Coping in cyberworld

'Coping is living in today's world. Whatever way you can.'

Amie, 17

Contents

Learning outcomes

The aim of this module is to facilitate students to actively apply learned coping skills from previous modules in day to day situations, especially when using the internet, to increase personal safety and to make safer choices online. By the end of this module students will have a general understanding and basic skills to deal with some common online issues.

In this session students will:

❀ Be able to identify risks and dangerous activities online
❀ Be able to start thinking about cyber-ethics through the means of 'Netiquette'
❀ Be able to identify the different types and forms of online harassments, especially cyberbullying
❀ Be able to identify some strategies and agencies where they can seek help when they encounter online harassment

Instructor's notes

Research suggests that the best prevention would be through education which optimizes adolescents' coping capacity when dealing with negative online events (Campbell, 2005; Lodge & Frydenberg, 2007). In 2004 the Canadian government developed an educational, computer-based programme which teaches students in Grades 7 and 8 about risk and safety issues associated with internet use (Ontario Physical Health Education Association, 2007). Evaluation of this programme yielded strong positive results. In 2008 a pilot study using much of the content of this module had found further positive outcomes.

Setting the context

This module will allow students to explore many real-life examples of negative online experiences they may encounter in their daily lives. To set the context of this session, it is useful to review Module 7 on problem-solving and to encourage students to use the more productive coping skills that they have learned. If working in a class or group, it is again important to emphasize the importance of confidentiality to increase students' comfort level and to facilitate the sharing of their thoughts.

Another important element in setting the context is the instructor. The instructor provides an invaluable model for positive thinking. Modelling a positive attitude and positive thinking within the group will help consolidate the topics discussed and reinforce the value of adopting a positive attitude.

Group and classwork activities

Ice breaker: Let's tok abt txt
Time: 10 minutes

Materials: Enlarged copy of Handout A on page 159, copies of Handout B on page 160 for all in the group, music, felt-tip pen, music

Instructions: This ice breaker requires a small amount of preparation. It works like 'Pass the parcel'. Ask the class to sit in a circle and pass the felt-tip pen around while music is playing. When the music stops, the student who is holding the felt-tip pen needs to attempt to complete one of the abbreviations listed on Handout A. When the activity is completed give all students a copy of Handout B.

Teaching tip

Language is the way we express ourselves, and it is constantly evolving over time. Take, for example, the comparison between 'thou' and the more modern use of 'you', which clearly demonstrates how different words are used in different contexts, and how this is also changing with the times. In our fast-paced society, time is gold. We try to be efficient with everything and, as a result, many commonly used phrases and words have been reduced and abbreviated to enhance how we rapidly communicate.

Text abbreviations online are known as internet acronyms. Handout A (questions) and Handout B (answers) will help you ensure students understand the terms and meanings of some common internet acronyms.

Internet acronyms are easily misinterpreted and difficult to keep up to date, as they are constantly being altered and created. Some of them become commonly used and some of them remain secret codes shared among certain groups of people. It is likely that students know other frequently used abbreviated phrases that are not included in this module and so student input should be encouraged.

Activity 1: The cyber savvy teens

Time: 30 minutes

Materials: The Cyber Savvy Teens Tipsheet on page 161

Instructions: Encourage students to share some of their negative online experiences. Ask them what they did when they encountered negative online experiences and what other ways they could deal with the same situations. Discuss with students ideas on how to be safe online. Provide students with a copy of the handout. Ask students if there are any other tips they can think of.

Activity 2: Delete cyber harassment

Time: 30 minutes

Materials: Scenario Cards (see page 165), the Cyber Event Thought Chart (see page 163) and Six Problem-solving Steps (see page 164)

Instructions: This activity is designed to better prepare students to deal with different situations they may encounter online. Help students to generate ideas that will help them to be cyber harassment proof. Use the problem-solving tasks as examples to help you achieve this goal. This activity can be done in small groups or with the entire class. Review with the students the Six Problem-solving Steps and use The Cyber Event Thought Chart as a problem-solving framework to assist you and your students to complete this activity. There are some questions in the Teacher Support Notes below for you to use to help your students generate some solutions for the presented scenarios. The Cyber Savvy Teens Tipsheet on page 161 may be helpful as well.

Teacher support notes

Scenario 1
How would Sean and Madeline feel?
What should Sean and Madeline do now that they found this website?

Scenario 2
What do you think Joey would feel?
What can Joey do now?
What can Joey do differently to prevent this happening?

Scenario 3
Did Annie make an informed decision when she chose to meet David?
Is Annie putting herself in a situation that is potentially dangerous to her personal safety?
How could Annie have handled this situation differently?

Scenario 4
What do you think happened in this situation?
What has Ben done and what should he do instead?

Scenario 5
What do you think happened?
Why is he feeling unusually tired?
What should Josh do?

Individual instruction and homework activities

Provide each young person with the tipsheet Hot Tip Number 10: Tips for Parents and Teachers on Cyber Harassment on page 166. Encourage students to distribute this to their parents or guardians. Allow sufficient time for this to be read and discussed.

Resources

These can be photocopied from the following pages
or downloaded from http://education.frydenberg.continuumbooks.com

Let's tok abt txt

There are a lot of abbreviations and short ways of expressing ourselves over mobile phones and the internet. Sometimes we assume that we know what abbreviations mean. Test yourself and see which ones you know. For example, 'B' refers to the word 'be', 'C' is 'see', '4' refers to 'for', and 'FAQ' means 'Frequently Asked Questions'. Are there other text words that you use on a frequent basis?

ATM	_____	SRY	_____
AKA	_____	M8	_____
ASL	_____	MYOB	_____
ASAP	_____	CYA	_____
B	_____	WOT / W@	_____
B4	_____	CU	_____
B/C	_____	C	_____
EZ	_____	NE	_____
PLS	_____	XO	_____
GR8	_____	OMG	_____
BTW	_____	L8R	_____
BFZ4EVR	_____	JK	_____
L8R	_____	DNR	_____
LOL	_____	OIC	_____
LULAS	_____	PPL	_____
DK	_____	R	_____
LUV	_____	F2F	_____
TTYL	_____	PRW	_____
4YEO	_____	SPK 2 U L8R	_____
IMO	_____	AFK	_____

Let's tok abt txt: answers

Let's talk about text

ATM	At the moment		SRY	Sorry
AKA	Also known as		M8	Mate
ASL	Age, Sex, Location		MYOB	Mind your own business
ASAP	As soon as possible		CYA	See you
B	Be		WOT/W@	What
B4	Before		CU	See you
B/C	Because		C	See
EZ	Easy		NE	Any
PLS	Please		XO	Hugs, Kisses
GR8	Great		OMG	Oh my god/Oh my goodness
BTW	Between		L8R	Later
BFZ4EVR	Best friends forever		JK	Just kidding
L8R	Later		DNR	Dinner
LOL	Laugh out loud		OIC	Oh I see
LULAS	Love you like a sister		PPL	People
DK	Don't know		R	Are
LUV	Love		F2F	Face to face
TTYL	Talk to you later		PRW	Parents are watching
4YEO	For your eyes only		SPK 2 U L8R	Speak to you later
IMO	In my opinion		AFK	Away from keyboard

The cyber savvy teens tipsheet

1. Do not share your personal information.

2. Keep your passwords private.

3. Be a healthy sceptic.

4. Never open a message from someone you don't know and never agree to meet someone you don't know.

5. Protect your computer. Use anti-virus, anti-spams and content filters.

6. You are in control! Save the messages (and record the date and time), do not respond to the messages, block the sender and close the window.

7. Internet is just another form of entertainment. You don't have to be on it 24/7. Computers can be fun, but they are nothing compared to having a happy real-world life and hanging out with friends!

8. Talk to a trusted adult when you are in doubt.

9. Report 'cyberbullying' to your internet providers, website servers, the local police and The Net Alert.

The cyber savvy teens tipsheet teacher resource

1. Do not share your personal information
   - Whatever is posted online is equal to placing the same information on an advertisement board publicly displayed on a major freeway for everyone to see. If students do not want their personal information to be known to the general public, they should not put it online.

2. Keep your passwords private
   - Student should be careful not to share their passwords. Do not use passwords that can easily be discovered, for example, your middle name or your pet's name. A well secured password should have at least 6 digits composed of both letters and numbers, for example 'NSC080'.

3. Be a healthy sceptic (worksheet is modified from Ontario Physical Health Education Association, 2007b).
   - Not everything online is real. The internet is an open space where everyone can post anything they like, any time of the day. It is important to carefully evaluate the credibility of the websites you visit. Have the students discuss how they can tell if information in a website is trustworthy. Report it to the relevant media authority if you find information on a website, chat room, forum or newsgroup offensive.

The cyber event thought chart

Identify the type of cyber harassment:

Who can help? Where can I seek help?

List the positive and the negative choice the characters made:

Identify a few ways you can stay safe on the internet:

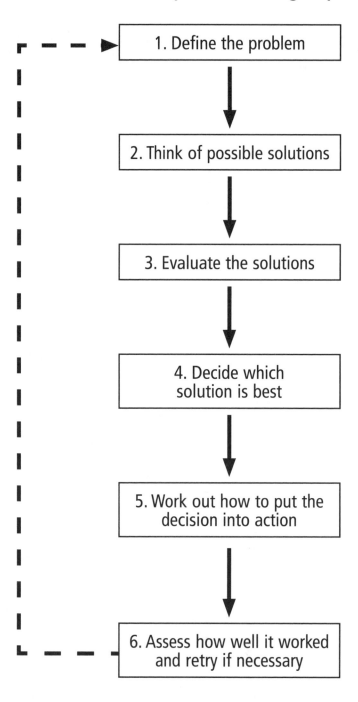

The six problem-solving steps

1. Define the problem

2. Think of possible solutions

3. Evaluate the solutions

4. Decide which solution is best

5. Work out how to put the decision into action

6. Assess how well it worked and retry if necessary

Scenario cards

Scenario 1
Some of the kids at Bayview Secondary School decided to set up an anonymous website expressing their views about different students in their school. The first page contains an internet polling survey listing the fattest and the ugliest boy and the sluttiest girl in Year 8. Photos were placed beside the names in the survey. Sean showed the site to his friend Madeline. Both of them are listed on the site.

Scenario 2
Joey joined a popular social networking site recently. In her profile, she gave her name, school, e-mail address and some school photos of herself and her friends. Recently she received a text message with a weblink sent to her from a good friend attending a different school. In that weblink, she found her photograph with a caption which took her school picture completely out of context. She also found other personal information of hers on the weblink.

Scenario 3
Annie joined an online chat room about local bands. The group discuss everything about bands (up-coming events, how to form your own band, performing opportunities, sharing new songs, and so on). She participates in many of the discussion threads. Lately Annie has been invited to chat privately with David, another member of the online group. Recently David has been talking about a lot more than playing electric guitar. He has been talking about wanting a girlfriend to hang out with, forming his band and finding a female lead singer for his own band.

David seems like a really nice guy and his online profile shows that there are many common interests between Annie and David. Annie decided to accept his invitation to meet at the local shopping centre. It's a public place so she knows she is safe. She told her good friend Sally that she would give her a full up-date after she meets with David. Annie promised Sally she wouldn't miss out any juicy details.

Scenario 4
Ben loves to play computer games online. As he plays his games, he chats with many people. When another player has defeated him, he gets very angry and uses vulgar language towards them. Ben later receives an e-mail from the online game server informing him that there are numerous complains about him being abusive during the online games and Ben is warned that he will be banned from the game if his behaviour persists.

Scenario 5
Josh recently received a gift from his mother. A new computer, with all the latest software, so he can play his favourite computer games and surf the net. Ever since he got his computer, Josh gets online as soon as he gets home from school, and he won't log off till the minute before he goes to school in the morning. Josh used to set a log-off time at around 9 o'clock at night, but that time would come and pass without him noticing. He finds himself feeling unusually tired and falling asleep in class. Josh's friends have commented on how they are not seeing Josh as much as they used to.

Tipsheet: Hot tip number 10: tips for parents and teachers on cyber harassment

Safety tips for parents and teachers to increase internet safety

1. *Education about safe and responsible use.* Implement prevention programmes as part of the school curriculum teaching young people what to do and what not to do online. Help students learn how to problem-solve.

2. *Code of conduct for use of technology.* Define appropriate internet use in school or at home with your child. For example, define appropriate websites and time spent on the internet. (see www.netsafe.org.nz or www.wiredsafety.org or *Real Wired Child* for examples of family internet contracts).

3. *Effective supervision and monitoring.* Apart from physical monitoring (for example, the occasional shoulder check), teachers can use computer software such as content filters and activate parental locks whenever it applies. These programs will help teachers to better protect young people from accessing inappropriate materials. (see www1.k9webprotection.com)

4. *Place the computer in a public place.* The computer should be placed in an open area within the classroom or home. Open areas are defined as a location where everyone in the room can view the computer user's activities.

5. *Communicate! Ask if you don't know.* The internet world changes rapidly, and young people's favourite online activities change quickly as well. If you don't understand, explore it with the student. Simply ask open-ended questions, such as, 'The game you are playing looks very interesting. Why don't you tell me more about it?'

Seven forms of cyberbullies (Willard, 2007)

1. *Faming.* Online fights using electronic messages with angry or vulgar language

2. *Harassment.* Repeatedly sending nasty, insulting and humiliating messages

3. *Denigration.* Putting down someone online. Spreading gossip or rumours about a person to damage the victim's reputation or friendship

4. *Impersonation.* Pretending to be someone else and sending or posting materials to get that person into trouble or danger or to damage that person's reputation or friendships

5. *Trickery and outing.* Sharing someone's secrets or embarrassing information or images online

6. *Exclusion.* Intentionally and cruelly excluding someone from an online group/community

7. *Cyberstalking.* Repeated and intense harassment and denigrating that includes threats or creates significant fear.

Guidelines for identifying youths who may experience cyberbullying

Observe any sudden changes in behaviour that might indicate problems related to internet use.
Examples:

- ❀ Be alert to sudden change of internet-usage patterns.
- ❀ Observe any sign of emotional distress such as moodiness, anxiousness, being unusually alert, panicking or experiencing difficulty in paying attention or concentrating, especially after use of the internet.

Let parents know about the students' signs of distress. Talk individually to students about their attitude or behaviour changes.

Do not judge. Students may hesitate to talk about what happened online. Most youths worry that no one will believe them. Students further worry that their internet privileges will be withdrawn if they report any kind of cyberbullying.

Be a good listener and be patient. Let the student know you are available to talk and you are willing to listen.

Empower the youth. For example:

- ❀ Let the student know it is not their fault they're being targeted by cyberbullies.
- ❀ Let the student know something can be done and there are people willing to help.

Find out what resources are available at your school and your local community. For example:

- ❀ Refer to school policy for guidelines on how to approach the incident.
- ❀ Seek consultations from the school psychologist, guidance counsellor, social worker or principal about students who seem to need outside help.
- ❀ Seek consultation from local authorities responsible for handling online harassment.

Guidelines to assist youths who may experience cyberbullying or cyber harassment

1. Preserve evidence. Evidence is essential to make a case, and help the local authorities to identify the bullies.
2. Contact service providers to stop or remove the materials.
3. Make use of the technology available to block the bully.
4. Report the bullying or harassment to the school and do not approach the bully alone.
5. In extreme cases, for example, where personal safety is concerned, contact the local police.

Internet safety advisory groups and support

Name	Country	Weblink
NetAlert	Australia	www.netalert.gov.au
Bullying. No Way	Australia	www.bullyingnoway.com.au
Cybersmart Kids Online	Australia	www.cybersmartkids.com.au
Netsafe	New Zealand	www.netsafe.org.nz
Netsmartz	USA	www.netsmartzkids.org
I-Safe	USA	www.isafe.org
Wired Safety	USA	www.wiredsafety.org
Common Sense Internet Safety	USA	www.commonsense.com
Child Exploitation and Online Protection Centre	UK	www.ceop.gov.uk/
Childline	UK	www.childline.org.uk
Bullying UK	UK	www.bullying.co.uk
Internet 101	Canada	www.internet101.ca
Cybersmart	International	www.cybersmart.org
Chat Danger	International	www.chatdanger.com
Teen Chat Decoder	International	www.teenchatdecoder.com
Translate Teen Language	International	www.transl8it.com
Child Helpline International	International	www.childhelplineinternational.org/

Internet related Issues – legal and other support

Organization	Weblink	Helpline
NetAlert	www.netalert.gov.au/	1800 880 176 (Interpreters available)
Australian Communications and Media Authority	www.acma.gov.au	Melbourne Central Office Tel: 03 9963 6800
Computer Crime & Intellectual Property Section (United States Department of Justice)	www.cybercrime.gov/	
Bully Police USA	www.bullypolice.net/	
Bullying UK	www.bullying.co.uk	

Coping quiz

1. List three steps to becoming a cyber savvy teen.
2. What would be a non-productive way of coping with a cyberbullying issue?
3. Identify two productive ways of coping with cyberbullying that you would implement in the future.

Further reading

Aftab, P. (1999), *The Parent's Guide to Protecting your Child in Cyberspace*. Maidenhead: McGraw-Hill Publishing Co.
Biggs, B. (2006), *Chatroom*. Melbourne: Micklind Enterprises.
Carr-Gregg, M. (2007), *Real Wired Child*. Camberwell: Penguin Australia
Johnson, S. (2004), *Keep Your Kids Safe on the Internet*. Columbus: McGraw-Hill.

Module 11 – Goal setting and goal getting

'Learning to cope is helpful as it allows us to perform tasks to the best of our abilities during stressful times.'

Harris, 17

'It is good to set goals. They help you to become a better person and if you achieve them, it gives you a sense you can complete things you set.'

Luke, 12

Contents

Learning outcomes

The aim of this module is to build awareness about the relationship between goals and achievement and to explore and set individual achievable goals.

   In this session students will:

- Reflect on the importance of goal setting and attainment in relation to long-term wellbeing and mental health
- Understand the concept of proactive coping
- Develop long-, medium- and short-term goals that are realistic and achievable.
- Be able to utilize visualization techniques
- Understand the concept of 'flow'

Instructor's notes

Goals are an essential component of general wellbeing and happiness. People who regularly make realistic and achievable long-, medium- and short-term goals tend to report feeling happier and more positive. Young people formulate goals on a day to day basis. These might include academic, social, familial or extracurricular, such as those relating to sporting or artistic activities. The concept of' 'flow' attributed to Mihaly Csikszentmihalyi (1997) refers to the experience of pleasure when activities are so enjoyable and engrossing that time seems to stand still. When in the pursuit of goals, despite heavy demands of preparation, training or rehearsal, there is often an experience of preoccupation and pleasure, that is flow.

Setting the context

Much of our coping is reactive, that is, we deal with situations as they arise. Goal setting and goal getting are about utilizing proactive coping strategies to plan, anticipate and prevent problems from occurring. Proactive copers build up their resources to move towards personal goals and strive to attain higher levels of performance. Their activities are purposeful.

Group and classwork activities

Ice breaker: Toilet paper praise

Time: 25 minutes

Materials: Two rolls of toilet paper

Instructions: Tell the students to take a length of toilet paper, allowing them to decide how much they take. Once each student has a piece of toilet paper in front of them, inform everyone that, for each square of toilet paper they have, they will need to say one positive thing about how they cope with difficult situations.

Activity 1: Windows to the future

Time: 25 minutes

Materials: Windows to the Future handout from page 180. Coloured felt-tip pens or pencils

Instructions: Provide students with the handout. Ask them to imagine that looking through each window will enable them to see themselves in the future at particular intervals of six months, one year and five years.

Their task is to draw what they see. They may use symbols, pictures, words or a combination of all three. Ask them to reflect on the possible things that may change during each of the time intervals.

Young people will be more inclined to focus on appearance. While this is certainly something they may like to represent, ask them to focus on some of the following areas:

❀ Personal physical growth (in relation to age at each point)
❀ Living arrangements
❀ Friendship groups
❀ Schooling, education or employment
❀ Environmental changes
❀ Interests, hobbies, activities in spare time
❀ Likes and dislikes

Once each window has been completed, ask students to sit in a circle and share their responses. Pay special attention to the variation in student responses and emphasize that goal setting and future directions are unique experiences. You may also wish to choose a specific example from a student's work to draw from and ask the group questions such as, 'What specific steps will be needed for (the student) to achieve this outcome or goal?'

As an extension of this activity, you could collect the student handouts at the end of the activity, ensuring that students have not recorded their names on the worksheet. Place all worksheets in the centre of the room, with students seated around the pile. Ask students to take in turns identifying which set of windows and goals match which student.

Activity 2: Heroes and heroines

Time: 10 minutes

Materials: Heroes and Heroines worksheet from page 181, a variety of magazines

Instructions: Divide students into small groups. Ask them to flip through magazines for inspiration and cut out pictures of celebrities or sporting heroes they find inspiring or talented. Ask each group to complete the worksheet. Once everyone has completed the worksheet, discuss student responses as a whole group. Ask students how they may apply lessons from their heroes to their own lives.

Activity 3: Setting achievable goals

Time: 15 minutes

Materials: A Guide to Setting Achievable Goals handout from page 181, pens or pencils

Instructions: Provide students with the handout and ask them to complete it individually. Once completed, ask them to share their responses with a partner.

Reflection

Ask students to reflect on a goal they have made in the past, preferably in the last 12 months. Ask them whether or not they achieved their goal. Can they identify why they were successful or why they were unable to achieve their goal? What would they do next time?

Individual instruction and homework activities

Prior to commencing the following activities, provide each young person with the tipsheet Hot Tip Number 11: Goal Setting and Goal Getting found on page 182. Allow sufficient time for this to be read and discussed.

Activity 11.1: Proactive coping

A. Consider the following situation:

Situation: John has set himself the goal of achieving 100 per cent for his English exam.

What could John do to maximize the likelihood of reaching his goal?

The week before his exam John realizes that he is having more difficulty in recalling a particular piece of text than he anticipated. Rather than getting stressed and anxious, what could John do to proactively cope with his difficulty?

B. Think about the goals you have set for yourself in the past. All of us have set ourselves goals in the past. They may have been to do with school, work, sport, music, health, behaviour or a variety of other things. You may have set goals in private – such as a commitment to yourself – in public – such as a New Year's resolution – or with just a couple of close others – such as with friends or parents. Sometimes they just don't work out!

What are some of the reasons why you have not achieved all of your goals?

Think of one goal that you have not achieved and write it down here.

How did you feel about the goal?

Activity 11.1: Proactive coping – continued

What happened to your motivation to achieve that goal?

_____

Now, look at a goal that you have set and achieved. The goal does not have to be earth-shattering. It may have been as simple as 'keeping my room clean' or 'not fighting with my sister'. What was the goal?

_____

What was the difference between this goal and the one that you did not achieve?

_____

What helped you follow through and achieve your goal?

_____

Activity 11.2: Exploring goals

Take some time to think about goals you would like to set and achieve in different areas of your life. Some goals might be small and achievable by the end of today, others may take you years.

A. At school

What are your short-term goals?

_____

What are your long-term goals?

_____

B. At home

What are your short-term goals?

_____

What are your long-term goals?

_____

C. Outside school and home

What are your short-term goals?

_____

What are your long-term goals?

_____

Activity 11.3: Elements of achievable goals

A. Think about a goal that you would like to achieve. Write this goal down.

_____

Keep this goal in your mind as you will be asked to refer to it throughout this module.

B. Recall your goal from above.

Is your goal realistic?

_____

Very large goals may be made more realistic by breaking them down into smaller goals.

_____

Break the above goal down into smaller goals.

_____

C. What effort will you make to achieve your goal?

_____

D. Does your goal fit in with other important things in your life? How will you balance your life?

_____

E. Now visualize yourself achieving your goal. Have a clear view of what you want to achieve and make sure you describe your goal in a positive way, for example, 'To eat healthier snacks such as fruit and nuts in between meals.' rather than 'To stop eating junk food.'

How do you describe your goal?

_____

F. A detailed plan is important. When making a detailed plan you will need to keep these basic ideas in your mind:

I want:

_____

I want it by (when):

_____

To achieve my goal I will have to do the following:

_____

I will know I have achieved my goal when:

_____

Activity 11.4: The concept of 'flow'
Time: 15 minutes

Materials: None

Instructions: 'Flow' is a subjective state that people report when they are completely involved in something to the point of total engrossment, when the activity becomes all-important. Examples include being engrossed in a novel, playing sport, having a conversation. and so on. The concept of 'flow' is used to explain how people remain engaged in activities that become satisfying in their own right. You lose track of time as the activity is intrinsically enjoyable. Musicians, sportspeople, artists and people who love what they are doing often report that time seems to stand still. Often these activities are part of one's goals.

Think about your hero or heroine.

- Do you think that they experienced 'flow'?
- In which endeavour?
- What is an activity that you enjoy doing so much that you lose track of time? Is it a leisure activity or does it contribute to achieving your goal?

Modifying the activities for students with additional needs

Gifted or high-achieving students often have goals that they strive to achieve vigorously. They are often tough on themselves if the outcome is less than perfect. There needs to be some discussion about the negative effects of self-blame and the need for reinforcing one's own achievements in a positive way: 'I have worked hard and done my best'. These students in particular need to learn to be kind to themselves and to use positive self-statements. When goals are not achieved how can they be reviewed and revised to have a greater likelihood of success?

Resources

These can be photocopied from the following pages
or downloaded from http://education.frydenberg.continuumbooks.com

Windows to the future

In six months' time

In one year's time

In five years' time

Heroes and heroines

Write down at least two people you admire:

Why do you admire these people?

What do you think they had to do to get to be the people they are today?

Would they have had to work hard or make any sacrifices?

If so, why would they have made those choices?

A guide to setting achievable goals

My goal is: To be achieved by:

GOAL

Look at your goal. Is it:
Realistic?
Achievable?
if not, revise your goal.

Remember, you are going to have to put in EFFORT to reach your goal.
Are there any changes to your lifestyle you will have to make? How will you BALANCE your life?

VISUALIZE your goal.
Think of your goal in positive terms.
Write or draw your positive goal.

I know I will have achieved my goal when:

To achieve my goal I will have to:

Activity	To be completed by	Date completed	Reward

Tipsheet: Hot tip number 11: Goal setting and goal getting

We set all different kinds of goals. Goals can be related to achievement, studies, hobbies, families and friendships.

When we set goals, we are making planned decisions and choices for our futures. Our goals direct our future actions. For example, if your goal is to save enough money to purchase a new CD player in two months, then you might stop purchasing magazines for the next few weeks to increase your savings.

Our goals tell us where we want to go. But in order to get there, we need to act in particular ways now and make decisions today that will help us. For example, it would be quite difficult to participate in an 8-km fun run if you had not set this as your goal and increased your fitness gradually.

Acting in ways that maximize the likelihood of reaching our goals is called proactive coping.

Elements of achievable goals

1. *Realistic.* Is the goal realistic?

   Very large goals may be made more realistic by breaking them down into smaller goals. For example, if your goal is 'to become a famous singer', it might seem that the road ahead is a long one. Break your goal down into a series of smaller targets. For example, taking singing lessons, joining the school choir, practising singing in front of small groups of people and performing on stage.

2. *Achievable.* Is the goal achievable?

   Goals need to be defined and specific so that you know when you have accomplished them. For example, if you wish 'to be a great hockey player', will you have achieved your goal when you are one of the best in your school team? One of the best in the local area? When you make it into your country's team? When you win an Olympic medal? You need to have specific outcomes in mind and specific time frames. 'Some time in the future' is not the sort of time frame that will motivate you to start working toward your goal.

3. *Effort.* Are you willing to put a lot of time and effort into achieving the goal?

   For example, you might fantasize about becoming a famous singer but be unwilling to put in the hard work, especially with the more boring aspects like undertaking vocal exercises.

4. *Balance.* Does the goal fit in with other important things in your life?

5. *Visualize.* Visualize positive goals.

   Visualization is a powerful tool. You need to have a clear view of what it is you want and how it will be when you achieve it. This will help to keep you on track and motivated for success. When setting goals, frame them **positively** instead of **negatively**. For example, if you want to stop snacking on so much junk food, your goal might be 'to eat fruit when I want a snack'. Then, imagine yourself eating fruit, enjoying it and feeling satisfied as well as getting the benefits of feeling healthy, having energy, clear skin, etc.

6. Accept the *responsibility.*

If you don't do something about it, it won't get done. It is up to you to direct your own life. You have choices about how to spend your time and what pursuits to follow. These choices will determine your future.

7. *Plan.* Make a detailed plan to follow.

Once you have defined and written down what you want, then write down the detailed activities you will need to undertake in order to achieve it. You will need a separate plan for each goal. For each goal there are likely to be many activities involved in the steps to achievement. For some of these you may be relying on other people.

8. And lastly...*review.*

As you work through your goal plan, look over it and review how your progress is going. Are you on the right track? Does your planning need some slight modifications? A major overhaul? Adjust as you go and learn from your own mistakes and successes for the best chance of achieving your goal.

Reward yourself. Don't forget to give yourself a pat on the back or small reward when you make even small gains. You decide when and how, and work this into your plan. Rewards can be as simple as participating in an activity you enjoy or telling someone of your success. Rewarding yourself and celebrating small steps along the way will motivate you to achieve your larger goal.

Coping quiz

1. Why are goals important to make and maintain?
2. What are the elements of a goal that make them successful?
3. How can you ensure goals are successful?

Further reading

Greenglass, E. R. (2002), 'Proactive coping and quality of life management'. In E. Frydenberg (ed), *Beyond Coping: Meeting Goals, Vision and Challenges*. New York: Oxford University Press, 37–62.

Schwarzer, R., & Taubert, S. (2002), 'Tenacious goal pursuits and striving toward personal growth: Proactive coping'. In E. Frydenberg (ed), *Beyond Coping: Meeting Goals, Visions, and Challenges*. New York: Oxford University Press, 19–36.

Module 12 – Time management

'If you want time, you must make it'

Anonymous

Learning outcomes

By the end of this module students will be able to evaluate how they spend their time and learn to manage it in effective ways.

In this session students will:

- ❀ Reflect on how time is spent
- ❀ Learn to break tasks down into component bits
- ❀ Develop strategies to avoid procrastination
- ❀ Develop a realistic timetable for achieving tasks

Instructor's notes

Managing time is a skill we all need. It is often about doing it better than we have done it before. Essentially all the coping skills considered in the earlier sessions are important in that we need to know what to do and what not to do when it comes to coping productively. Additionally the skills required in goal setting and goal getting, as well as in decision-making, are important assets to help one manage time better. Anticipating what might come in the way of smooth sailing is important. That is, skills of planning and proactive coping are helpful.

While adults know that managing time efficiently and effectively is important, young people are less likely to appreciate that fact. It is therefore important to engage them with the problem of how best to achieve what needs to be done in the timeframe that has been set or is available.

Setting the context

'Time stands still for no-one' is a saying that can mean different things for different people but generally it means that time is valuable and we need to manage it well. Often when it is not managed well it means that there is too much to do and too little time. The problem needs some problem-solving skills and some skills of decision-making. Where shall I start? What stops me from starting? Do I do the things I like best first so as to get into the task or do I start with my least favourite activities first and then get onto the easier or more pleasurable ones? Getting started is often the big challenge. Getting it done on time is about management of time. Being proactive rather than reactive is about being able to plan in a realistic fashion, deciding how long will it take and anticipate hurdles and interruptions. What resources will be required and how one goes about getting the resources such as the assistance of others are important considerations.

Group and classwork activities

Ice breaker: Scavenger hunt
Time: 10 minutes

Materials: Two envelopes containing instructions

Instructions: Divide the group into two teams – the red and the blue – and give each team an envelope with a set of instructions. For example, find as many people as you can who can roll their tongue into a U-shape; find as many people as you can with a younger sibling. Give the group 10 minutes and then process how the group managed their time. How did they organize themselves to be efficient?

Activity 1: How do I spend my time?

Time: 10 minutes

Materials: None

Instructions: Divide the group into pairs. Ask students to reflect on how they spend their time. On a typical school day, what are the out of school activities that they do? How do they spend their time at the weekend? How do they separate work and leisure? How do they structure their time at home? When do they have to structure their own time, for example, when doing homework? Or family chores?

At the end of the activity ask, 'What did you learn about yourself?' 'What did you learn about your partner?'

Activity 2: Breaking the task into manageable bits

Time: 10 minutes

Materials: Whiteboard and whiteboard markers

Instructions: Explain to the students that most activities can be broken down into components. For example: if students were to begin a project on the environment, such as water conservation, they may need to ask themselves:

- ❀ What aspect of the topic would I like to explore?
- ❀ What is the sequence in which I address the topics?
- ❀ Where do I start the search for information? Going to the library? Turning on the computer?
- ❀ When does it have to be finished?
- ❀ Which bits do I do when?

Ask the group of students to think of various tasks that they may engage in. Record the list of tasks on the whiteboard. Analyse with the group what components of each task need to be tackled to ensure the task is completed.

Task to be completed	Components that have to be tackled

Activity 3: Getting started

Time: 10 minutes

Materials: Whiteboard, whiteboard markers, pencil and paper for each student

Instructions: Explain to the group that difficulties in getting started can be a result of different things. Some students may think to themselves: Is the task daunting? Have I got too much to do? Am I afraid that I will fail?

These concerns often lead to indecision, procrastination and avoidance activities. Procrastination has been around for a long time. 'Procrastination is the thief of time' is a saying attributed to Edward Young (1683–1765).

Using the whiteboard, demonstrate to the students the following positive and negative thinking patterns that discourage and encourage procrastination, respectively.

Encouraging procrastination	Overcoming procrastination
Self-downing	**Positive self-statements**
I'll do it tomorrow	Today is a good day to draw up the plan
I like to work under pressure	I can break the task into bits
I am hopeless at getting onto things	I will draw up a realistic timetable
I always leave things until the last minute	I will start with an achievable bit that I like
It is only worth doing if I can do it perfectly	It is better to get started and then I can revise and improve it if necessary
There is no-one that can help me	Any effort is better than none
	I can find someone to give me a hand

Ask students to draw up the following table and complete it. Allow students a sufficient amount of time to complete the table. Instruct students to form pairs and discuss their thinking statements. Ask students to discuss how these thoughts may influence their behaviour and feelings.

Encouraging procrastination	Overcoming procrastination

Reflection

Ask students to reflect on the way they use time and think of common sayings to do with time. Examples might be 'a bird in the hand is worth two in the bush', 'a stitch in time saves nine', and so on.

Individual instruction and homework activities

Prior to beginning the following activities, provide each young person with the tipsheet on page 193. Allow sufficient time for this to be read and discussed.

Activity 12.1: Awareness of time spent

A. In the table list the things you did yesterday and the time spent on each. For example, eating, watching television, sport, homework.

Event/activity	Time spent

How well do you think you managed your time yesterday?

B. Think of the things you have to do in the next seven days. For example, finish an assignment, visit a relative, clean your room. List four things here:

C. How will you deal with interruptions?

D. Think about what your priorities are. Recall your 'things to do list' from above. Look down your list and prioritize your tasks, from the most to the least important. Or you may like to mark each task with the following:

A = Urgent, must do today

B = Important, but not essential today

C =This can wait (you can make up a heading to suit yourself)

Prioritize your 'to do list'. List the things you have to do in order of importance:

Activity 12.1: Awareness of time spent – continued

_____

_____

E. How will you manage your time?

_____

F. How can you say NO to people without being rude?

_____

G. Complete the following timetable for the next week:

Tasks	Importance	Priority#	To be completed by	Who to ask if help is needed

Modifying the activities for students with additional needs

Students with additional needs may experience significant diffficulty in regulating their behaviour and engaging in time management and organizational skills. Often, in order for young people with additional needs to be successful in time management, a diary, schedule or timetable needs to be devised for them. For a student with learning difficulties, consider the use of a visual schedule. A visual schedule is a sequence of pictures, symbols or words used to inform a young person of the events they will be undertaking throughout the day or within a particular time period. Schedules are designed to provide information, reduce anxiety and provide contingency over less desirable activities (e.g., a student may see that first they have maths, then they have a break).

Visual schedules may be displayed using:

- Wonderwall boards
- Whiteboards (drawings, numbers, words)
- Photo albums (or business-card holders)
- Keyrings (belt)
- Desktops
- Key chains (neck)

Various software packages exist in which materials can be made to suit the individual needs of the students. Some examples are:

- **Boardmaker** from Mayer Johnson is a graphics database containing over 3,000 Picture Communication Symbols (from PCS Books I, II, & III) in bitmapped clip art form. The program allows you to make communication displays, quickly find and paste pictures, print displays and make worksheets, picture instruction sheets, reading books, journals or posters. http://www.mayer-johnson.com
- **Picture This** from Silver Lining Multimedia 914-462-8714 is primarily designed to make flash cards and lotto boards in 2,400 photo-quality images and works with Boardmaker. http://www.silverliningmm.com/
- **Flash, Flash Pro, and Flash Pro2** Each CD contains between 5,000 and 8,500 colour photographs that can be made into flash cards. http://shops.looksmart.com/aba
- **Pics for PECS (Picture Exchange Communication System)** Pyramid Educational Consultants Books, video and materials. http://www.pecs.com

Time management helpers need not necessarily be 2D. Helpers that you may already own include an egg timer, electronic kitchen timer, talking stick, whiteboard or blackboard.

Resources

These can be photocopied from the following pages
or downloaded from http://education.frydenberg.continuumbooks.com

Tipsheet: Hot tip number 12: Time management

Managing your time well is essential to be able to fit in all the things that you need or wish to do, both day to day and from week to week.

Goals and good planning are essential to effective time use. You need to have in mind what it is that you need to achieve (English essay due Thursday) and set aside the required time (well before Thursday!) that will allow you to achieve this goal without stress and that means you won't be trying to write the essay quickly on Thursday morning just before your English lesson.

Some simple guidelines to manage time include:

1. Be proactive rather than reactive. Learn to anticipate and plan for stress.
2. Plan your time. Try not to let events and other people push you beyond your limits. Be assertive and make your limits clear. Be aware of your own stress levels.
3. Plan quality time. Find uninterrupted time to focus on a task and do only one at a time.
4. Find out your own best time for working. Accept this rhythm in yourself and use it to your best advantage.
5. Be realistic about what you can do. Don't put demands on yourself with which you are unlikely to be able to cope. Be honest with yourself and others.
6. Be aware of how you spend your time. Monitor yourself for a day or two and write down everything that you do. Have you spent your time wisely?
7. Set long-term goals as well as short-term goals and prioritize.

What are your priorities?

Facing a long list of tasks can increase your stress and confusion and it may just seem easier not to do any of them! However, you will find that there are some things on the list that:

❀ Are more important than others
❀ May be able to be completed another day
❀ May be able to be done by others
❀ You may be able to ask for extra time to complete.

For example, if it's your turn to do the dishes and you don't have much time, you may be able to make a deal with your sister. If she does them tonight, you'll do them on Saturday when it's her turn. You need to look down your list and prioritize your tasks. You may list them in order of importance, from the most important to the least, or you may like to mark them:

A = Urgent, must do today

B = Important, but not essential today

C = This can wait

(Or make up your own headings to suit yourself)

Very important and demanding tasks will need more time spent on them than unimportant or trivial tasks.

Coping quiz

1. In your own words describe why time management is important.
2. Name three negative thoughts that may encourage procrastination.
3. Name three positive thoughts that may prevent procrastination.

Further reading

Allen, D. (2001), *Getting Things Done: the Art of Stress-Free Productivity*. New York: Viking.

Morgenstern, J. (2004), *Time Management From The Inside Out: The Foolproof System for Taking Control of Your Schedule—And Your Life* (2nd ed). New York: Henry Holt/Owl Books.

Notes

2   Morton Deutsch, the 'father' of mediation and conflict resolution research, gave a famous example of two young people, a brother and sister, who have a conflict over an orange. Each wants the one orange that is available. But then, one day, when they talk about their interests and make it clear what they really want, it turns out that the girl wants the peel of the orange to make marmalade and the boy wants the inside of the orange to eat. So, once they understood their true interests, the conflict disappeared.

3   Remember the difference between needs and wants.

SECTION 3

Coping skills for particular groups

In this section the adaptations of the 12 modules that may be made for diverse populations of young people are described. It is possible to conduct the programme with a particular group, such as those who have experienced loss or family separation, as the members of any group with a shared experience may help and support each other when they consider matters of relevance. However, groups of young people, such as those who have experienced parental separation, are participants in the general school community and sometimes it is not advisable to isolate individuals with particular needs but to include them in a universal programme so that those with particular needs can benefit from the discussion and experiences of those who are coping well.

Nevertheless it is important to understand the needs of particular groups of young people, such as those who have experienced loss, as they are often well represented in the general population. One of the benefits of small group instruction, which is generally the way special needs are met, is that participants report that they enjoy talking to peers who share similar experiences or concerns. The participants are likely to feel less alone with their difficulties and can benefit from the sharing of experiences and learn from the different ways that each member of the group may have dealt with their situation or concern.

For each of the groups described in this section there is information about their characteristics, their particular needs and the ways that it is helpful to think about coping for that population. Where we have research evidence on coping skills intervention for that group that will also be cited. Following is consideration of the groups, namely, adolescents who have a learning disability, young people who have experienced loss, divorce, depression, chronic illness or Asperger's Syndrome. Finally, there is a general discussion about small group instruction.

The groups and the topics discussed are by no means comprehensive but, rather, are provided as a stimulus for ideas that can be incorporated into teaching and may be adapted for other groups.

Learning disabled

Students who have specific learning disabilities

Students with specific learning disabilities (SLD) are presented constantly with challenges. Failure to develop expected reading, spelling or mathematics skills frequently results in negative labelling and exclusion from participation in some aspects of school life. These students are at risk of passivity, disruptive behaviour and social withdrawal. A major determinant for success for students with SLD is whether they are likely to be able to cope adaptively with their learning disabilities (Firth, Frydenberg & Greaves, 2008; Rodis, Garrod & Boscardin, 2001; Westwood, 2008)

Features of the population

While there is debate about what constitutes specific learning disabilities, it is helpful to think of a person with specific learning difficulties as having:

> an IQ score greater than 80, and deficits in at least one area of academic achievement (reading, spelling, mathematics) associated with specific cognitive impairments, such as short term memory problems, poor auditory discrimination ability, visuo-perceptual problems, and the like (Prior, 1996, 4).

The prevalence according to the above definition indicates that one in ten young people is likely to be affected. It is considered to be a lifelong phenomenon and genetically based. There are associated esteem- and confidence-related impacts for the individual. Recently attention has become more focused on compensation than remediation. The capacity to develop a feeling of empowerment for this population is important. Coping skills contribute to that sense of personal capacity. Some very highly successful individuals have done well in our Western communities despite experiencing specific learning disabilities. One internationally recognized success story is that of Richard Branson, the founder of Virgin Atlantic Airways.

Adapting the programme

In one study Firth (2006) adapted a coping skills programme for 98 adolescents in years 7–9, aged 12–16 years, with learning disabilities, that is, students who were two or more years below the expected level for age in reading, spelling or mathematics. Programme modules were comprised of materials relating to choice of coping strategies, positive thinking and assertiveness training and were conducted over 11 weekly sessions. There were frequent revisions of the concepts and there was a revision component at the start of each session.

Practice activities were developed as between-session reinforcers, much as those that have been designed for individuals as part of the 12 modules in this book. For the learning disabled group the practice activities involved rehearsal of skills relating to students' personal goals, weekly discussion of progress made towards achieving the set goal and use of graphs to measure progress with targeted skills. Inclusion of role-play activities provided further opportunity for intensive, multi-modal revision of strategies. The personal goals, which related to both academic life and non-academic life, provided opportunity for revision and generalization of programme strategies beyond the classroom environment.

Students with specific learning disabilities are frequently very able in areas that do not require the specific reading, writing or mathematical skills with which they have difficulty. Students' written responses were replaced by drawings, oral responses and role-play. Reading was also reduced to a minimum. All print-based handouts were modified or removed. Where appropriate the teacher read a script while two students took on the role of negative or positive thinkers and the class orally contributed their responses as to the feelings these thoughts provoked. The worksheets contained only a few key sentences or phrases (Firth, 2006).

The focus of the intervention for this group particularly related to taking control of the situation and being assertive. Thus, when the concepts of coping were introduced, taking control was emphasized. There were three sessions on positive cognitive reframing, or positive self-talk, as negative self-talk is how these young people generally cope. Within the context of problem-solving the assertiveness skills were also taught, as learning disabilities were seen as a problem that needed to be solved or dealt with but also had to be managed in a confident and assertive way.

Evaluation

In the Firth study participants from four schools were divided into four groups who received either the coping programme, a teacher-feedback programme, both the adapted coping programme and a teacher-feedback programme or who acted as a wait-list control group. The teacher-feedback programme involved teachers giving individual feedback to students which focused on finding and using a strategy in response to a particular difficulty. The programmes were implemented at each school by the classroom teacher. The coping programme and teacher-feedback programme teachers participated in professional development sessions of approximately two hours' duration and the coping programme teachers received a manual. Teachers of both programmes were also given on-site weekly support. Duration of the interventions was generally ten weeks, with the coping programme occurring for one 50-minute session per week. The teacher feedback occurred within core class lessons without increased time allocation. All groups undertook pre- and post- programme and ten-week follow-up questionnaire completion.

What learned

Of the two interventions the coping programme was associated with the most definitive change in the study. However, at follow-up the coping group reported an increase in the productive coping strategies of working hard and working at solving the problem. Significant positive changes in internal perceived control were also reported at follow-up for the coping programme group only.

This outcome, and the qualitative responses of students and teachers, indicated that the content and processes that made up that coping programme were effective. The participants valued assertiveness, positive thinking and problem-solving. Teachers also indicated that the programme resulted in improved relationships with students, gave assistance with difficult classes and resulted in them feeling more competent in assisting students who had specific learning disabilities.

The researcher reported that a particularly interesting benefit of the programme was the development of a shared language of coping between students and teachers. This may be particularly beneficial in enabling teachers and their students who have specific learning disabilities to discuss what has previously been referred to as these students' 'behaviour problems' under the more inclusive language of coping (Firth, Frydenberg & Greaves, 2006).

Previous experience would suggest that a coping skills programme should be made longer for this group, with many opportunities for training and reinforcement. Class-based instruction could be supported by a computer-based programme that does not require extensive reading and which engages the student interest through the different format. A self-paced computer format, such as *Coping for Success* (Frydenberg, 2007), may encourage students to work more on their new skills in environments outside of school.

Children who have experienced divorce

The group

Young people today experience numerous challenges and opportunities as they progress through childhood and adolescence. Many of the experiences are similar to those their parents would have encountered, such as school transitions, puberty, friendship hurdles, illnesses and injuries. However, there are also challenges and opportunities of the modern world, such as parental divorce or separation, which are much more common for children today than in any generation before (deVaus & Gray, 2004; Wise, 2003).

Parental separation marks a significant turning point in the lives of all immediate family members. It often occurs after a period of dysfunction or family conflict. Additionally, children are required to adapt to a variety of subsequent changes, such as moving home and possibly school, shared custody or the absence of one parent. Parents may be unavailable to fully support their children due to their own emotional distress. Common feelings for young people who experience parental separation are confusion, sadness and isolation. Many adolescents, females in particular, can think they are to blame and feel guilty (Laumann-Billings & Emery, 2000; Rice & Dolgin, 2002). Some boys and girls, however, perceive their parents' separation as a relief, especially if there had been conflict within the marriage.

Even months or years after the separation, young people are required to cope with a variety of situations that young people from intact families do not experience. For example, living between two homes, maintaining contact with a parent who does not live at home, a parent's remarriage and the possibility of adjusting to a blended family (Zill, Morrison, & Coiro, 1999). Young people with separated parents are by no means less able to cope or succeed in life. Rather, they must learn to cope exceptionally well to manage the added challenges of having separated parents and to be able to think positively about the opportunities the separation makes possible for all family members.

For this group coping programmes can provide training in the strategies that will assist them to navigate their lives and respond to challenges in productive ways. Participants gain confidence in their ability to manage future obstacles. There are different ways of reaching young people and providing such intervention. While a universal class-based coping skills programme may be appropriate for this group a small group intervention may provide additional peer support. Young people report that the realization that they are not alone is most helpful.

Ivens (2006) delivered a coping skills programme to 27 girls in small groups of five to six girls who were aged 13 and 14 years. All had experienced parental divorce or separation. The small group context allowed the programme to be sensitive to the needs of the individuals within the group. Being able to discuss personal experiences and attach productive coping strategies to these increased participants' learning and applicability to the real world. The unique situation of each girl revealed itself throughout the programme, yet the coping strategies learned were appropriate for all. For example, one girl used the problem-solving steps to determine how to get along better with her mother's partner, and another to decide with which parent to celebrate her birthday that year. The level of emotional support among participants and peer modelling would have been difficult to foster in a whole-class programme.

How adapted

Several adaptations were made for the delivery of a coping skills programme for girls with separated parents.

The small group context enabled the programme to best meet the needs of this group of participants. It also served to enhance participants' sense of belonging and connection with each other and enabled the girls, in this case, to bond through the sharing of personal experiences and allowed girls to learn from each other. A climate of openness and trust was established early in the programme. The examples used related to complexities of having separated parents. A session on coping with conflict and taming anger, much the same as appears in Module 6, was used. Research indicates that young people with separated parents may have, and continue to have, a substantial amount of conflict in their lives (Sun, 2001). Indeed, issues relating to conflicts with peers and family members were raised by many participants. The participants appeared to benefit from the explicit teaching of conflict resolution and anger management strategies, both of which are important aspects of productive coping.

At the conclusion of the programme Ivens suggested that there be a parallel parent intervention. Because changes in behaviour and relationships often require the commitment of both parties, there could be a parent component that runs parallel to the adolescent programme. This would be true for any coping skills programme. For this particular group parents could receive information with the goals of strengthening post-separation parenting, parent–child relationships and coping. Information could be provided via a parenting programme or during one or more information evenings. A particular difficulty would be the group delivery for estranged parents and thus previous interventions for parents have deemed it necessary to offer such programmes to custodial parents only (Dawson-McClure, Sandler, Wolchik, & Millsap, 2004).

A programme may require additional tailoring for boys, such as the inclusion of more practical or physical activities and intensive facilitation to elicit the verbal expression of emotions. Within a mixed group, girls could possibly act as important role models in emotional expression. A programme could be tailored to focus on adolescents who have recently experienced parental separation (less than one year) and on those who experienced it some time ago (more than one year). For example, coping with grief, loss, rapid change and acute stress may be an important aspect of a coping programme for the former group, but less imperative for the latter group.

What found

Ivens' study provides promising evidence that a coping skills programme can be an effective intervention for adolescent girls who have experienced parental separation. Generally Ivens found that productive coping went up and non-productive coping went down. More particularly the strategies that went up included problem-solving, physical recreation and focusing on the positive. The strategies that decreased in usage were worry, not coping, tension reduction, self-blame and keeping problems to one's self. Additionally on the general health questionnaire there were demonstrated improvements, as there were in the students' attitudes to their parents' divorce. This study highlighted the benefits of teaching coping skills in small groups, with skilful instruction to an appropriately targeted group.

Ivens reported that programme benefits were far-reaching, including the fact that girls were able to make positive changes in how they managed their emotions and coped with situations and relationships both at home and at school. The girls felt safe to share their stories and explore their coping with each other, which highlighted the power of reciprocal learning. Being part of a small group allowed for openness and trust, and endorsed the fact that there were others like them, that they were not alone.

Dealing with depression

What is depression?

Depression is more than just feeling sad or having a 'down' mood. It generally presents as a cluster of symptoms that occur at the same time. It often coexists with other disorders such as anxiety, conduct disorder, substance abuse and delinquency. Adolescent psychopathology is generally marked by the coexistence of disorders in addition to depression and the tendency for several emotional and behavioural problems to cluster or co-occur in the same individual is widely recognized. Furthermore, the presenting problem is sometimes only symptomatic of the underlying problem. For example, depression may be an outcome of the loss of a relationship.

Depression is an inner subjective experience that can be reported by the depressed person or observed by others through their behaviour. There are many stressors that lead to depression. Adolescents who are depressed give strong clues by their words or their actions. Depression, in a clinical sense, on the other hand, is manifested by five or more of the following [4]:

* Depressed mood
* Markedly reduced interest or pleasure in most activities
* Significant weight loss or weight gain
* Insomnia or hypersomnia
* Psychomotor agitation or retardation
* Fatigue or loss of energy
* Feelings of worthlessness or excessive guilt
* Reduced ability to concentrate or indecisiveness
* Recurrent thoughts of death or suicidal ideation

Prevalence rates vary but a range of 5–10 per cent of the population are likely to experience depression needing psychiatric treatment or psychosocial intervention at any one time in Western communities such as the UK, USA and Australia (WHO, 2007). Not all people will have the same symptoms and not all people will have all of the above symptoms. The severity of depression can vary. The symptoms of depression are thought to be due to changes in natural brain chemicals called neurotransmitters, which send messages from one nerve cell to another in the brain. Depression often means that the brain has fewer of these chemical messengers such as serotonin, a mood regulating brain chemical.

There is no single cause of depression but it often involves a complex interaction of biological, psychological and social factors. However, if the depression is reactive it is often helpful to identify the cause, when that is possible.

Depression can often be a response to a situation when something very distressing has happened, particularly if one cannot do anything to control the situation such as [5]:

* Past trauma or abuse, e.g. child sexual abuse, physical abuse, etc
* Current trauma or abuse, e.g. domestic violence
* Relationship break-up
* Having an accident that results in disability
* Significant loss, e.g. death of a loved one
* Developing a long-term physical illness (or caring for someone with an illness)
* Being a victim of crime

Depression can also occur from:

- ❀ A medical condition, e.g. diabetes
- ❀ The side-effects of certain medication/drugs
- ❀ The stress of having another mental health issue, e.g. severe anxiety, schizophrenia
- ❀ Alcohol abuse or drug abuse
- ❀ Changes in hormone levels
- ❀ Lack of exposure to bright lights in winter (Seasonal Affective Disorder)

Some people will experience depression in a distressing situation whereas others may not. Some people may be more prone to it whereas other people may be more resilient. Studies have shown that those most prone to developing depression are women, people with depression in the family and people who have experienced abuse during childhood (sexual, physical or emotional).

What are the effects of depression?

The manifestations of depression which may, in fact, be the precipitating factors or the outcomes include sadness and crying, withdrawal, mood swings, guilt, anger, feelings of helplessness and hopelessness, lack of emotional responsiveness, loss of interest in appearance, lack of motivation, neglect of responsibilities, overeating or loss of appetite and self-harm. Depressed young people often blame themselves (more common in girls) or blame others (more common in boys). The single most important indicator is a person acting 'out of character', that is, differently than usual. For example, the usually exuberant active person becomes quiet and withdrawn.

The things depressed people say to themselves

'It's all my fault'; Worry: 'What if…'
Suicidal ideation: 'The world would be better off without me'
Pessimism: 'Everything sucks'
Confusion: 'I can't think straight'
Self-doubt: 'I can't do anything'
Self-hatred: 'I'm disgusting' and a concern that others are judging one: 'They wouldn't like me if they really knew me'

Intervention

When developing a programme to assist depressed individuals it can be helpful to include a discussion about depression and, in particular, what it is, what the effects are, how to recognize it in someone and where to go for help.

While it is not helpful to group any number of depressed young people together, there is strong evidence that when depressed young people are in a universal group programme they are likely gain more benefits from the programme that the rest of the group. However, the principles inherent in the coping skills programme and the sessions can and have been used with individual young people who are depressed, with very promising results.

In this section we mention the various components of coping instruction that are recommended for emphasis because they are likely to be particularly helpful to depressed young people.

When working with an individual, particularly as a trained counsellor, it is important to identify the real problem. It is helpful to determine whether it is a reactive depression such as those listed above, and/or one that requires a systemic intervention, such as teasing and bullying in the school context. It could also be a problem that the individual needs to tackle with a range of resources, which may include personal resources, such as coping skills, or external resources such as family- or school-related supports.

If a student is depressed and is being supported by a coping skills programme it is generally wise to have an expert counsellor involved. The particular issues for that student can be addressed and the goals of a coping skills development programme can be established. One of the goals could be to assist the individual to identify and access supports that are deemed to be helpful in dealing with the situation. An important part of the intervention would be to help change the individual's thinking through Rational Emotive Techniques or Cognitive Behavioural techniques. Providing problem-solving skills, so that the problem is not resolved by the support person but rather by the individual as the problem-solver, is empowering.

A Rational Emotive Behaviour Therapy (REBT) and Cognitive Behavioural Therapy (CBT) approach can be used to address negative/irrational thinking. This Cognitive Behavioural approach for treatment of stress and depression is based on an assumption that psychological problems are manifested from maladaptive patterns of thinking (Ellis, 1957; McMullin, 2005). Both REBT and CBT as action-oriented approaches to coping are most helpful, as is a person-centred approach, which can underpin the helping process (Rogers, 1983). Person-centred therapy aims to provide a climate conducive to growth and therapeutic change. According to Rogers, this is achieved through the implementation of genuineness, empathy and unconditional positive regard (Kahn, 1997). Furthermore, behavioural-based strategies can be employed so that motivation through intrinsic and extrinsic reinforcement is fostered to maintain commitment to change (Carr & Durand, 1985).

One strategy which is helpful to all students, and particularly helpful to depressed young people, is to draw or use a cardboard cut-out of the 'helping hand' and ask the student to write on each finger a person to whom he/she could talk to if they had any worries or concerns (see page 95). Once completed, this will act as a visual tool for encouraging help-seeking behaviours. Creating a pathway to connectedness with friends, family and school is considered to be a fundamental to promoting wellbeing and resilience in students. Secondly, challenging self-talk is helpful. An example is given below of a student, Tani, who was depressed, living away from home in a boarding-house setting.

A. Think of something that has happened to you that made you feel upset or disappointed in yourself:

What happened?   I really did badly in maths

What did you think?   I am dumb

How did you feel?   Stupid, sad

B. Evaluate your self-talk:

Was it 100 per cent accurate?

Were there other possibilities?

Possible reasons self-talk may be true: I really got a poor result

Possible reasons self-talk may be false: I usually do well in maths

Recall your old thought(s) from above: I am dumb

New thought(s): I am not dumb but sometimes I get bad marks in maths

The Emotion Meter is also a good technique for helping young persons to identify the intensity of their feelings. The meter can be drawn from 1–10 or 1–100 and the feelings can be positive or negative, using emotion words.

To consolidate the concept of challenging thoughts, an activity can involve the formulation of rational thinking cards. A series of rational thoughts are written on strips of paper and spread across the table. These rational thoughts include (see Hajzler & Bernard, 1991, 135):

* Just because things are not succeeding today does not mean I'm a no-hoper or that I will not succeed tomorrow
* While it is very desirable to achieve well and be recognized by others, I do not need constant achievement and recognition to survive or be happy
* Mistakes and rejections are inevitable. I will work hard at accepting myself while disliking my mistakes and knockbacks
* My performance at work – imperfect or otherwise – does not determine my worth as a person
* Things are rarely as bad, awful or catastrophic as I imagine them to be
* I accept who I am
* There are many things about me that I like and do well
* I am confident that everything will turn out okay given that I have my goals, know what to do and work hard

From the above series of rational thoughts the student can select those that apply to them and write them on a card.

The REBT strategy can be dealt with individually or within the group as all members would benefit.

What happened?   What were you thinking?   How did you feel?

The students can be asked to identify which of the coping strategies they would like to improve and then identify how they would action the strategies that they have selected. For example, Tani chose the following:

1. Seek social support

   Talk to room-mate

   Talk to mum

   Talk to teacher

   E-mail friends overseas

2. Work hard and achieve

   Make a study timetable

   Remember that I am good at maths. This is my strength.

   Ask for help when I need help. People I can ask are…

3. Focus on solving the problem

   Practise problem-solving, following these steps:

   1. State what the problem is

   2. Brainstorm ways of solving the problem

   3. Choose the best option

   4. Try out the option

   5. Check how well I did in solving the problem

4. Seek relaxing diversions

   Start yoga

   Go to meditation on Fridays

5. Seek professional help

   The school counsellor

   General practitioner

   Kids' helpline

   Lifeline

6. Physical recreation

   Walk to the shops and back every night

   Yoga

   Bike ride at weekend

Then Tani was helped to use the problem-solving model to deal with her particular problem and work out how she would move from one school to another.

Problem-solving model

Steps	Actions
State the problem	I am worried about starting a new school
Brainstorm ways of solving the problem	Ask lots of questions Research my new school E-mail the administration officer with some questions Make contact with the school counsellor
Choose the best option	A lot of those option are good, but we could start with e-mailing the administration officer a list of questions
Try out the option	Yes
How well did you do?	She replied and my questions were answered

The outcome for the student for whom the programme was adapted resulted in a smooth transition to another school where she was able to establish contacts and support systems with the aid of a counsellor prior to making the move.

Helping a young person with depression

Generally the family doctor is a source of assistance as appropriate referrals can be made through him/her to other professionals and medication provided as deemed necessary. There are many websites with information and support for depression. International organizations such as LifeLine are likely to have branches in most major cities and can be readily found on the internet.

Chronic illness

Features of the population

Chronic illness is one that lasts for a substantial period or that has consequences that are debilitating for an extensive period of time. It generally interferes with daily life for longer than three months or requires hospitalization (Boice, 1998). These illnesses include asthma, diabetes, lupus, cystic fibrosis, cardio-vascular diseases, HIV and other sexually transmitted diseases. While most of these chronic diseases require ongoing management, in the past many of these diseases would have resulted in shortened life expectancy. Today many of these young people survive into, and through, adolescence. The conditions can tax both the individual's and the family's resources, often resulting in relationships of over-dependence on the part of the adolescent or over-involvement on the part of the parent. Often family tension is a feature of these relationships.

Additionally there are issues that relate to peer acceptance. Biological issues related to the timing of puberty emerge. For example those with Crohn's disease, cystic fibrosis and chronic renal disease may have a later than average entry into puberty. Perception of the adolescent's physical appearance and physical capacity may psychologically impact how the individual feels about himself or herself. There are uncertainties relating to treatment outcomes and life expectancy that can lead to anxiety. Sexual issues may also add to anxiety. Given that achieving autonomy and independence are important milestones in adolescence, restrictions in that regard can be quite stressful.

While the management of the different illnesses requires different coping strategies on the part of the family and the individual, the reality is that there are a range of issues that adolescents with a chronic illness have to deal with that are additional to those managed by adolescents in general.

Overall when reviewing the literature on chronic illness Meijer, Sinnema, Bijstra, Mellenbergh and Wolters (2002) make the point that that chronically ill adolescents do not generally cope differently with illness-related stressors than they do with their other stressors. It is not so much the diagnosis as the chronicity of the condition. These researchers collected data from 84 adolescents and the coping style they found to be of most relevance to adjustment was what they called 'confrontational coping' which was characterized by active and purposeful problem-solving and the adequate use of social skills, along with the absence of anxiety in social situations (although to a lesser extent) and the use of assertive behaviour. They point out that this was in line with the results that they found in an earlier study with healthy adolescents. Overall their work has highlighted the utility of an active coping style which includes a healthy use of social support.

Schmidt, Petersen & Bullinger (2003) make the point that coping and development are inextricably linked in that coping varies according to age and stage of development and coping in turn impacts development. Coping in chronically ill adolescents remains stable over time (Spirito, Stark, Gill, & Tyc, 1995). That is, the implication is that young people draw upon a set of coping strategies that remain part of their repertoire. While there are several ways to assess how young people cope with a specific illness, it is quite appropriate to use a general form of a coping questionnaire, or for example, to use the Specific form of the Adolescent Coping Scale and relate the coping strategies to the particular condition. Using the items of the ACS enables the adolescent to focus more sharply on his or her particular coping strategies and reflect on what they utilize a lot or a little in order to cope with their illness.

One study compared 47 8–13-year-olds with asthma, 52 with atopic dermatitis and 57 with cancer to 58 healthy controls matched by gender and age on self-report of academic and interpersonal stressors (Hampel, Rudolph, Stachow, Lab-Lentzsch & Petermann, 2005). Academic stressors included items such as 'when something at school bothers me I am really worried, e.g., taking a difficult exam or dealing with too much homework', while interpersonal stressors include items such as 'when other children are bothering me I am really upset, e.g. a conflict with peers or malicious gossip expressed by peers'. Coping with everyday stressors was improved for early adolescents suffering from one of the chronic diseases compared to their healthy controls. Those adolescents with a chronic disease used less passive avoidance on cross-situational coping and more situation-specific coping with social- and school-related stresses. Cross-situational coping was obtained by calculating mean scores across data on coping with both stress situations.

In another study with an older age group (12–15 years) a sample of 521 students suffering inflammatory bowel disease, chronic liver disease, congenital disease, coeliac disease or food allergy were compared to 245 healthy controls. They used the Coping Inventory for Stressful Situations (CISS-21), which has been used frequently with children experiencing chronic disease. In that study there was no difference between diagnostic groups nor between diagnostic groups and the controls (Calsbeek, Rijken, Bekkers, van berge Henegouwen & Dekker, 2006). There are indications that young people who experience chronic stresses due to illness appear to be able to harness their coping resources in order to manage adequately their illness and the stresses that such circumstances inevitably present. Thus the weight of evidence indicates that young people with chronic illnesses are generally highly resourceful and utilize a good range of productive coping strategies. However, the principle that we can always do what we do better holds for this group as well as for a universal population.

Adaptation of the programme

For each of the chronically ill groups, a generic coping skills programme, much the same as is described in this book, is likely to be helpful. The issues most relevant to the group need to be identified. For example, for young people who are managing diabetes the issue might be to maintain a regimen that requires self-monitoring of behaviour. For this, as for many other groups, the issue of managing time, with the additional demands placed on them through the need to manage their health, is an important consideration.

The examples in each of the modules of the programme need to be tailored to the particular condition being dealt with, that is, the sessions need to be condition specific. The examples need to be engaging in that they need to be seen as genuine problems to be solved and thus perceived to be relevant. When it comes to chronic illness, as with some other groups, it is generally helpful to bring young people together. In situations like that they can get the legitimacy of their concerns affirmed, realize that they are not alone with the problem and can also be of great assistance to each other in management of their concerns.

When students are coping with chronic illness, as with anything that is important and time-consuming, the issue of engagement in a programme and maintenance of interest is most important. Activities that are perceived to be fun need to be employed. Acting and role-play suit some groups and some individuals, but for others it is the more visual or personalized verbal exchanges that are most useful. Humour is always helpful and young people with chronic illness often use humour to deal with their situation. Eliciting humorous situations that individuals have experienced can assist with group bonding and these situations can then be discussed in relationship to coping. How did you cope? What worked? What would you do differently? Asking the group how they might have dealt with the situation or would in future deal with the situation can also be helpful.

In a current study being conducted at the University of Melbourne (Serlachius, 2009) young people with diabetes will receive a ten-session coping skills programme, with the above recommendations incorporated into the programme. It is expected that the programme will help participants to adhere to their regime better than they would with a regular diabetes management programme alone. Attendance will be encouraged through ongoing communication between the facilitator and the participants. This will be done through weekly e-mails or text-messaging to remind the adolescents of their next session as well as to encourage and support them between sessions. Another option that is being explored, and which can be used for any group, is the development of an online social networking forum that can be used to communicate with the group facilitator or with the other group participants.

Young people with Asperger's Syndrome
Particular needs of students who have Asperger's

Young people with Asperger's Syndrome are a group who generally have needs over and above that of the general population, particularly in relationship to social skills. They are a group who do not intuitively distinguish between what is appropriate behaviour and what is not. They have been identified as needing extensive social and emotional skill development. Because of their inappropriate social skills they are also often the victims of bullying.

Features of the population

Asperger's Syndrome is one of the autism spectrum conditions and reflects the way an individual communicates and relates to people around him or her. It is a lifelong developmental disorder that is considered to fall on the mild end of the autism spectrum disorders continuum (Barnhill, 2007). Asperger's is characterized by difficulties in social interactions, in the social use of language and in imaginative thinking. The lack of imaginative thinking relates to rigid and inflexible thoughts, where things are viewed from the person's perspective and there is an inability to understand or imagine the views of others. Other characteristics include poor motor skills and spatial awareness, poor executive functioning (i.e. organizational and planning skills, impulse control, self-monitoring, time management, and the adoption of new strategies) and sensory overload where excess noise, colour, smell or movement may cause anxiety and distress.

The difficulties experienced by young people with Asperger's can lead to anxiety and depression (Attwood, 2007).

Asperger's Syndrome affects three to four times as many males as females. It can occur with varying severity. Superficially these young people have good verbal skills and do not have intellectual disabilities. Thus, generally in the school setting, an adolescent with Asperger's is integrated into the classroom where they often appear aloof or indifferent, making approaches to others only when wanting to meet physical needs, accepting the approaches of others passively and sometimes making bizarre one-sided approaches. There can be a marked impairment in the ability to initiate or sustain a conversation with others. The key features of Asperger's Syndrome are:

- Cognition may be high average to superior on standardized assessments
- Often language skills are good and performance skills are poor[6]
- Often there exist specific learning difficulties

Students:

- Are rule driven
- Are concrete thinkers
- Are rigid decision-makers
- Often appear to lack common sense
- Have limited problem-solving skills
- Have difficulty transferring learned information and skills to new situations
- Have limited ability to explain their own behaviour
- Cannot predict or understand the behaviour of others
- Love number-based activities, science and rule-based learning
- Have good concentration on topics of interest

The diagnostic criteria for Asperger's Disorder in DSM IV (American Psychiatric Association, 2000) is a qualitative impairment in social interaction, as manifested by at least two of the following:

- Marked impairment in the use of multiple non-verbal behaviours, such as eye-to-eye gaze, facial expression, body postures and gestures to regulate social interaction
- Failure to develop peer relationships appropriate to developmental level
- A lack of spontaneous seeking to share enjoyment, interests or achievements with other people
- Lack of social or emotional reciprocity

Restricted repetitive and stereotyped patterns of behaviour, interests and activities as manifested by one of the following:

- Encompassing preoccupation with one or more stereotyped and restricted patterns of interest that is abnormal either in intensity or focus
- Apparently inflexible adherence to specific, non-functional routines or rituals

🌼 Stereotyped and repetitive motor mannerisms (e.g. finger flapping or twisting or complex whole-body movements)

🌼 Persistent preoccupation with parts of objects

Adaptation of the programme

Given what we know about young people with Asperger's, there are deficits that need to be addressed. Generally these deficits relate to social skills that are likely to be helpful for all young people. However, it is the extension of the social skill and problem-solving related activities that needs to be considered. Rather than teaching these activities in one session it is likely that numerous repetitions and examples will need to be created so that there are the requisite number of reinforcements for skill building to be achieved. In general terms the emphasis is on building social skills, the capacity to recognize one's body language, gaze, eye contact and body stance and translate these into appropriate learnt behaviour.

Module 2 and Module 3 which address the relationship between our thoughts and feelings are important for young people with Asperger's Syndrome as they are prone to worrying too much and thinking in a negative and self-critical way.

Module 4 on getting along with others is also relevant as people with Asperger's Syndrome who have difficulties in navigating their social world, in particular, the ability to predict other people's behaviour and to understand the consequences and impact of their own behaviour on others.

The modules that examine strategies for making decisions, goal setting and managing time will also benefit people who have deficits in organizational and planning abilities, time management, prioritizing and adapting or implementing new strategies.

Participants with Asperger's will need to learn to initiate a conversation and have a two-way conversation (This can be done by extending Activity 3 in Module 8, see page 133). Generally, social and group activities are likely to be difficult but provide an excellent skill-development platform. Additionally these students will require numerous examples and multiple reinforcements in the social–emotional domain.

These students enjoy number-based activities and can sustain concentration on topics of interest, so examples and activities that interest the students need to be developed. This is true of all students, but more so for this group. For example, if trains are of interest then the problem-solving or the social problem-solving situation can include an example of a train-related activity.

If Asperger's young people are going to participate in a universal setting then it is likely that they will have good social role models in the group. Since they are concrete thinkers, the modelling and role-play examples need to be explicitly presented as exemplars. If that is not possible then the instructor can model the social skills. Similarly the instructor can demonstrate inappropriate behaviour. As part of the social skills training cooperative and competitive games should be encouraged. Students can also be encouraged to join organizations that involve social contact and represent their interests. Reading and discussion of biographies and autobiographies can also be used to encourage empathy. When dealing with emotions explore only one emotion at a time. Encourage the use of a diary, letters and poetry to express emotions and drama and music to extend emotional comprehension.

Asking for help (Module 5) is also a strategy which needs to be taught for this group. How to recognize that one needs help and how to approach someone and initiate a request is an important skill. The skills of self-awareness are likely to be difficult, as is the skill of making an approach to someone in person or via a telephone. A concrete list of resources that are appropriate for the problem and are available in the community need to be identified and made explicit. The role-plays and the rehearsals can then be used to make approaches to these settings.

Working in small groups

Young people often value the opportunity to work in a small group setting and will self-refer to a programme that is appealing if given that option. Two programmes with small groups of self-referred young girls have provided numerous insights as to what works and what does not. The most frequently voiced comment after such programmes is that it was found to be helpful to spend time in the small group as it offered the opportunity for both interpersonal exchange and personal reflection in a safe environment.

While the reasons a small group is set up are diverse, these generally include issues involving relationships that participants need help to manage. The sessions on dealing with anger and conflict are most useful (see Module 6) and can be extended in such a group. Students need to feel comfortable in the group and they need to be able to trust the group. Very clear statements need to be made, pointing out that what is said in the group stays in the group. This is true for all groups but more so for small groups where greater self-disclosure may occur.

In several such programmes conducted with girls, a session has been included that deals with identifying emotions. Familiar emotions are discussed and a comprehensive list is generated and compiled in a group setting. These emotions can then be grouped according to whether they represent positive or negative feelings and whether these are of high or low intensity. How are the positive emotions encouraged, that is, positive reframing? How are the negative one's regulated? What are the self-statements that can be learned? For example, normalizing the reaction if it is one of sadness and loss, with statements such as 'It is ok to feel sad when I have lost…'

An activity that has been added to the emotion session is one that has the students outlining a human form that represents their body and locating the part of the body where the particular emotion is experienced. The image in Module 6 (see page 109) can be used. By locating the seat of the emotion for the individual the person is then generally more readily able to identify the emotion and subsequently regulate it better.

While the relationship between thoughts and feelings is emphasized throughout the modules, the small group is an ideal forum to reinforce this. A visual representation of a circle for the head and one for the body can be used to illustrate the relationship between thoughts and feelings. Adding arms and legs to the circle representing the torso enables a focus on actions. As the emotions are located on a particular part of the body the linking of thoughts to feelings and actions can be represented diagrammatically. The image can be personalized and referred to on subsequent occasions.

In a small group session it is also possible to accommodate to the students' particular learning style. Some students, for example, prefer to write while others prefer to act out or draw situations. In a small group these preferences can be more readily accommodated.

Thus, whether the small group is self-selected, gender specific or one that targets young people with a particular need, it can be an ideal way for the professional running the programme to develop familiarity with the content and experiment with various adaptations.

Concluding remarks

The good news is that coping skills can be learnt, whether as part of a universal class-based programme, in a small group setting for young people with particular needs or for an individual. Skills are developed through experience, therefore opportunities for rehearsal play an important part. The more support that is provided for the group leader or for the individual participants to acquire skills, the greater the motivation and maintenance of momentum. Familiarity with content is strongly recommended before the commencement of the programme. It is important to affirm that theoretically there is no finite list of coping strategies just as there is no predetermined range of situations in which individuals find themselves.

So the creative instructor will draw upon the experience of the group and adapt or expand the materials provided in this volume to suit the skills and needs of the group, as well as drawing on their on experiences. As with all education, successful implementation is dependent on the commitment and enthusiasm of the instructor. The experience should be rewarding both for the students and the programme leader.

Notes

4   DSM-IV-TR, American Psychiatric Association (2000)
5   The modules can be adapted for individual or group application for any of these groups of young people.
6   Asperger's young people often have good receptive and expressive language skills but struggle with the pragmatic use of language. This includes the use of social niceties, inability to read non-verbal cues and a tendency to apply a literal meaning to words, therefore not being able to understand innuendos, analogies and humour.

References

American Psychiatric Association (APA) (2000), *Diagnostic and Statistical Manual of Mental Disorders*, Fourth edition text revision (DSM-IV-TR). Washington, DC: American Psychiatric Association.

Attwood, T. (2007), *The Complete Guide to Asperger's Syndrome*. London: Jessica Kingsley Publishers.

Barnhill, G. (2007), 'Outcomes in adults with Asperger's Syndrome.' *Focus on Autism and Other Developmental Disabilities*, 22(2), 116–126.

Beck, A. (1993), *Cognitive Therapy and the Emotional Disorders*. New York: Penguin.

Boice, M. (1998), 'Chronic illness in adolescence.' *Adolescence*, 33(132), 927–939.

Burns, D. E. (1999), *The Feeling Good Handbook*. New York: Plume.

Calsbeek, H., Rijken, M., Bekkers , M. J. T. M., van Berge Henegouwen & G. P. & Dekker, J. (2006), 'School and leisure activities in adolescents and young adults with chronic digestive disorders: impact of burden of disease.' *International Journal of Behavioral Medicine* 13, 121–130.

Campbell, M. A. (2005), 'Cyber bullying: An old problem in a new guise?' *Australian Journal of Guidance & Counselling*, 15(1), 68–79.

Cannon, W. B. (1932), *The Wisdom of the Body.* New York: Norton.

Carr, E. G., & Durand, V. M. (1985), 'Reducing behaviour problems through functional communication training.' *Journal of Applied Behaviour Analysis*, 18(2), 111–126.

Chesire, G., & Campbell, M. (1997), 'Adolescent coping: Differences in the styles and strategies used by learning disabled students compared to non-learning disabled students.' *Australian Journal of Guidance and Counselling*, 7(1), 65–73.

Cohen, J. A., Deblinger, E., & Mannarino, A. (2004), 'Trauma-focused cognitive-behavioral therapy for sexually abused children.' *Psychiatric Times,* 21(10), 221–228.

Cohen, J. A., & Mannarino, A. P. (1998), 'Interventions for sexually abused children: initial treatment findings.' *Child Maltreatment*, 3, 17–26.

Compas, B. E. (1987), 'Coping with stress during childhood and adolescence.' *Psychological Bulletin*, 101 (3), 393–403.

Connor-Smith, J. K., Compas, B. E., Wadsworth, M. E., Thomsen, A. H., & Saltzman, H. (2000), 'Responses to stress in adolescence: Measurement of coping and involuntary responses to stress.' *Journal of Consulting and Clinical Psychology*, 68, 976–992.

Csikszentmihalyi, M. (1997*), Finding Flow.* New York: Basic Books.

Dawson-McClure, S. R., Sandler, I. N., Wolchik, S. A., & Millsap, R. E. (2004), 'Risk as a moderator if the effects if prevention programs for children from divorced families: A six-year longitudinal study.' *Journal of Abnormal Child Psychology*, 32 (2), 175–188.

deVaus, D. A., & Gray, M. (2004), 'The changing living arrangements of children: 1946–2001.' *Journal of Family Studies*, 10(1), 9–19.

Doidge, N. (2007), *The Brain That Changes Itself: Stories of Personal Triumph From the Frontiers of Brain Science*. New York: Penguin Books.

Ellis, A. (1957),'Rational psychotherapy and individual psychology.' *Journal of Individual Psychology*, 13, 3–44.

Ellis, A. & Harper, R. A. (1975), *A New Guide to Rational Living*. North Hollywood: Wilshire Books.

Faust, J., & Katchen, L. B. (2004), 'Treatment of children with complicated posttraumatic stress reactions.' *Psychotherapy: Theory, Research, Practice, Training*, 41(4), 426–437.

Firth, N. (2006), 'Success despite learning difficulties.' *The Australian Journal of Learning Disabilities*, 11(3), 131–137.

Firth, N., Frydenberg, E. & Greaves, D. (2008), 'Perceived Control And Adaptive Coping: Programs For Adolescent Students Who Have Learning Disabilities.' *Learning Disabilities Quarterly*, 31(3), 151–165.

Firth, N., Frydenberg, E. & Greaves, D. (2006), 'Shared needs: teachers helping students with learning disabilities to cope more effectively.' In R. Lambert and C. McCarthy (eds.), *Understanding stress in an age of accountability*. Greenwich: Information Age Publishing, 65–87.

Folkman, S. & Lazarus, R. (1988), 'The relationship between coping and emotion: Implications for theory and research.' *Social Science Medicine*, 26 (3). 309–317.

Freud, S. (1964), 'The neuro-psychoses of defense.' In J. Strachey (ed and translator), *The standard edition of the complete psychological works of Sigmund Freud*. London: Hogarth, pp. 45–61. (Originally published in 1894)

Frydenberg, E. (2007), *Coping for Success*. University of Melbourne's eShowcase website: http://eshowcase.unimelb.edu.au/eshowcase/ and Melbourne: Australian Council for Educational Research.

Frydenberg, E. (2005). *Tough Minded and Tender Hearted: The Life and Work of Morton Deutsch*. Bowen Hills: Australian Academic Press.

Frydenberg, E. (2008). *Adolescent Coping: Advances in Theory, Research and Applications*. London: Routledge.

Frydenberg, E., Care, Freeman, E., & Chan, E. (In press). 'Interrelationships between coping, school connectedness and wellbeing.' *Australian Journal of Education*.

Frydenberg, E., Eacott, C., & Clark, N. (2008), 'Teaching Coping Skills: From Distress to Success.' *Prevention Researcher*, 8–12.

Frydenberg. E. & Lewis, R. (1993a), *Manual: The Adolescent Coping Scale*. Melbourne: Australian Council for Educational Research.

Frydenberg, E. & Lewis, R. (1993b), 'Boys play sport and girls turn to others: Age gender and ethnicity as determinants of coping.' *Journal of Adolescence*, 16, 252–266.

Frydenberg, E., & Lewis, R. (2000), 'Teaching coping to adolescents: When and to whom?' *American Educational Research Journal,* 37, 727–745.

Frydenberg, E. & Lewis. R. (2002), 'Adolescent well-being: Building young people's resources.' In E. Frydenberg (ed) *Beyond Coping: Meeting Goals, Vision and Challenges*. Oxford: Oxford University Press, 175–194.

Frydenberg, E., Lewis, R., Kennedy, G., Ardila, R., Frindte, W., & Hannoun, R. (2003), 'Coping with concerns: An exploratory comparison of Australian, Colombian, German and Palestinian adolescents.' *Journal of Youth and Adolescence,* 32, 59–66.

Galton, F. (1883*), Inquiries into Human Faculty and its Development*. New York: AMS Press.

Gray, C. (1995), *Social Stories and Comic Strip Conversations: Unique Methods to Improve Social Understanding*. Arlington: Future Horizons, Inc.

Greenglass, E. R. (2002), 'Proactive coping and quality of life management.' In E. Frydenberg (ed), *Beyond Coping: Meeting Goals, Vision and Challenges*. New York: Oxford University Press, 37–62.

Hajzler, D. J. & Bernard, M. E. (1991), 'A review of rational-emotive education outcome studies.' *School Psychology Quarterly*, 6, 27–49.

Hampel, P., Rudolph, H., Stachow, R., Laß-Lentzsch, A. & Petermann, F. (2005), 'Coping in children and adolescents with chronic diseases.' *Anxiety, Stress, and Coping*, 18, 145–155.

Hobfoll, S.E. (1998), *Culture and community*. New York: Plenum Press.

Huxley, L., Freeman, E., & Frydenberg, E. (2007), 'Coping skills training: Implications for practice.' *The Australian Educational and Developmental Psychologist*, 24(2), 44–68.

Ivens, C. (2006), 'The Best of Coping program: Small group counselling for adolescent girls who have experienced parental separation or divorce.' Unpublished Master's Thesis. Melbourne: The University of Melbourne.

James, W. (1892), *Psychology*. New York: Henry Holt and Company.

James, V. H., & Owens, L. D. (2004), 'Peer Victimisation and Conflict Resolution Among Adolescent Girls in a Single-sex South Australian School.' *International Education Journal*, 5, 37–49.

Kahn, M. (1997), *Between Therapist And Client: The New Relationship* (revised edn). New York: W. H. Freeman and Co.

Kendall, P. C. (2000), *Cognitive-Behavioral Therapy for Anxious Children: Therapist Manual*. Philadelphia: Temple University.

King, N. Tonge, B. J., Mullen, P., Myerson, N., Heyne, D., Rollings, S., Ollendick, T. H. (2000), 'Sexually abused children and post-traumatic stress disorder.' *Counselling Psychology Quarterly*, 13(4), 365–375.

Lam, C. (2008), Coping in the Cyberworld: Program Implementation and Evaluation. Master in Educational Psychology Research Project: University of Melbourne.

Largo-Wight, E., Peterson, P. M., & Chen, W. W. (2005), 'Perceived problem solving, stress, and health among college students.' *American Journal of Health Behavior*, 29(4), 360–370.

Laumann-Billings, L., & Emery, R. E. (2000), 'Distress among young adults from divorced families.' *Journal of Family Psychology*, 14(4), 671–687.

Lazarus, R. S. (1974), 'The psychology of coping: issues of research and assessment'. In G. V. Coelho, D. A. Hamburg & J. E.

Adams (eds), *Coping and Adaptation*. New York: Basic Books, 249–315.

Lazarus, R. S. (1991), *Emotion and Adaption*. New York: Oxford University Press.

Lazarus, R. S. & Folkman, S. (1984), *Stress, appraisal and coping*. New York: Springer.

Lewinsohn, P. M., & Clarke, G. N. (1999), 'Psychosocial treatments for adolescent depression.' *Clinical Psychology Review*, 19, 329–342.

Lodge, J., & Frydenberg, E. (2007), 'Cyber-bullying in Australian schools: profiles of adolescent coping and insights for school practitioners.' *Australian Educational and Developmental Psychologist*, 24, 45–58.

McMullin, R. E. (2000), *The New Handbook of Cognitive Therapy Techniques*. New York: Norton & Company.

McMullin, R. E. (2005), *Taking Out Your Mental Trash: A Consumer's Guide to Cognitive Restructuring Therapy*. New York: W.W. Norton & Company.

McTaggart, H. (1996), 'Students at risk of school exclusion: How they cope.' Unpublished Master's Thesis: University of Melbourne.

Meichenbaum, D. (1977), *Cognitive Behaviour Modification: An Integrative Approach*. New York: Plenum Press.

Meichenbaum, D. (1994), *A clinical handbook/ practical therapist manual for assessing and treating adults with post traumatic stress disorder*. Ontario: Institute Press.

Meijer, S. A., Sinnema, G., Bijstra, J. O., Mellenbergh, G. J., & Wolters, W. H. G. (2002), 'Coping style and locus of control as predictors for psychological adjustment of adolescents with chronic illness.' *Social Science and Medicine*, 54, 1453–1461.

Noto, S. S. (1995), 'The relationship between coping and achievement: A comparison between adolescent males and females'. Unpublished Master's Thesis: University of Melbourne

Olsson, C. A., Bond, L., Burns, J. M., Vella-Brodrick, D. A., & Sawyer, S. M. (2003), 'Adolescent resilience: a concept analysis.' *Journal of Adolescence*, 26, 1–11.

Ontario Physical Health Education Association. (2007). *CyberCops an Interactive Internet Safety Program*. Retrieved October 2008, from http://ophea.net/ophea/Ophea.net/ upload/njmfe.ppt#534,1,CYBERCOPS

Parsons, A., Frydenberg, E., & Poole, C. (1996), 'Overachievement and coping strategies in adolescent males.' *British Journal of Educational Psychology*, 66, 109–114.

Powell, T. (2000), *The Mental Health Handbook*. Milton Keynes: Speechmark Publishing.

Prior, M. (1996). *Understanding specific learning difficulties*. London: Psychology Press.

Rice, F. P., & Dolgin, K. G. (2002), *The Adolescent: Development, Relationship and Culture* (10th ed.). Boston: Allyn & Bacon.

Rickwood, D., Deane, F. P., Wilson, C. J., & Ciarrochi, J. (2005), 'Young people's help seeking for mental health problems. *Australian e-Journal for the Advancement of Mental Health*, 4, 22–33.

Rodis, P., Garrod, A. &. Boscardin, M. L. (2001), *Learning Disabilities And Life Stories*. Boston: Allyn & Bacon.

Rogers, C. (1983), *Freedom to learn for the 80s*. Columbus: Charles Merrill.

Rutter, M. (1994), 'Stress research: Accomplishments and tasks ahead.' In R. J. Haggerty, R. R. Sherrod, N. Garmezy and M. Rutter (eds), *Stress, risk, and resilience in children and adolescents: Processes, mechanisms, and interventions*. Cambridge: Cambridge University Press, 354–386.

Schmidt, S., Petersen, C., & Bullinger, M. (2003), 'Coping with chronic disease from the perspective of children and adolescents: A conceptual framework and its implications for participation.' *Child: Care, Health and Development*, 29(1), 63–75.

Schwarzer, R., & Taubert, S. (2002), 'Tenacious goal pursuits and striving toward personal growth: Proactive coping.' In E. Frydenberg (ed), *Beyond coping: Meeting goals, visions, and challenges*. New York: Oxford University Press, 19–36.

Seligman, M. (1992), *Learned Optimism*. Sydney: Random House.

Selye, H. (1976), *Stress in Health and Disease*. Reading: Butterworth.

Serlachius, A. (2009). 'Health and coping in type 1 diabetes: The effects of a psycho-educational program to improve metabolic control in adolescents with type 1 diabetes.' Ph.D, Dissertation Proposal: University of Melbourne.

Shiraldi, G. R. (2001), *The Self-Esteem Workbook*. West: New Harbinger Publications.

Skinner, B. F. (1953), *Science and Human Behavior*. London: Collier-MacMillan Ltd.

Smith, P., Perrin, S., & Yule, W. (1999), 'Cognitive behaviour therapy for post-traumatic stress disorder.' *Child Psychology & Psychiatry Review*, 4(4), 177–182.

Spirito, A., Stark, L., Gill, K. M., & Tyc, V. L. (1995), 'Coping with everyday and disease-related stressors by chronically ill children and adolescents.' *Journal of the American Academy of Child and Adolescent Psychiatry*, 34(3), 283–290.

Stallard, P. (2002), *Think Good – Feel Good. A Cognitive Behaviour Therapy Workbook for Children and Young People*. Chichester: John Wiley and Sons.

Sun, Y. (2001), 'Family environment and adolescents: Well-being before and after parents' marital disruption. A longitudinal analysis.' *Journal of Marriage and Family*, 63, 697–713.

Taylor, S., Klein. L., Lewis, B. P., Gruenwald, T. L., Gurung, R. A., & Updegraff, J. A. (2000). 'Biobehavioural responses to stress in females: tend-and-befriend, not fight-or-flight.' *Psychological Review*, 107, 411–429.

Weinberger, D. R., Elvevag, B., & Giedd, J. N. (2005), *The Adolescent Brain: A Work in Progress*. Washington, D.C: The National Campaign to Prevent Teen Pregnancy.

Weissberg, R. P. (2007, December), 'Social and emotional learning for student success.' Paper presented at the CASEL Forum 'Educating all Children for Social, Emotional and Academic Excellence: From Knowledge to Action.' Chicago.

Westwood. (2008), *What Teachers Need to Know About Learning Difficulties*. Camberwell: ACER.

Willard, N. (2007), *Educator's Guide to Cyberbullying and Cyberthreats*. Available at: http://www.cyberbully.org/cyberbully/docs/cbcteducator.pdf. Accessed 2 September 2008.

Wise, S. (2003), 'Family structure, child outcomes and environmental mediators: an overview of the development in diverse family study.' Research paper No. 30. Melbourne: Australian Institute of Family Studies.

Wolpe, J. (1958), *Psychotherapy by Reciprocal Inhibition*. Chicago: Stanford University Press.

World Health Organization (2007) http://www.who.int/topics/depression/en/. Retrieved 20 April 2009.

Youngs, B. B. (1985), *Stress in Children. How to Recognize, Avoid and Overcome it*. New York: Arbor House.

Zill, N., Morrison, D. R., & Coiro, M. J. (1999), 'Long-Term Effects of Parental Divorce on Parent–Child Relationships, Adjustment, and Achievement in Young Adulthood.' *Journal of Family Psychology*, 7(1), 91–103.

Zimmer-Gembeck, M., & Skinner, E. (2008), 'Adolescents coping with stress: Development and diversity.' *The Prevention Researcher*, 15(4), 3–7.